Wisconsin's Best: 365 Unique Adventures

The Essential Guide to Unforgettable Experiences in the Badger State (2025-2026 Edition)

Travel with Jack and Kitty

with

Kitty Norton

with

Jack Norton

Contents

Chapter 1

Introduction

Welcome, friend, to a journey like no other; a journey into the heartland of America, where the air is crisp and the cheese is in a league of its own. Prepare yourself for an adventure through Wisconsin's vast rolling farmlands, majestic forests, and bustling urban landscapes that retain a distinctive, friendly small-town feel.

This is your guide to 'Wisconsin's Best: 365 Unique Adventures,' an essential compendium of unforgettable experiences in the Badger State.

Despite its reputation as America's Dairyland, Wisconsin's appeal reaches far beyond its renowned cheese factories and cow-dotted pastures. The state's rich history and diverse geography, coupled with its vibrant cultural scene, and world-class culinary offerings, ensure an experience that thrills the senses and satisfies the soul. And of course, there's the undeniable charm of the Wisconsinites themselves, a friendly, welcoming people who embody the spirit of Midwest hospitality.

Wisconsin is a four-season destination, each season presenting its unique beauty. Springtime brings blooming wildflowers, lush landscapes, and migrating bird species that turn the sky into a mesmerizing canvas. Summers are for shimmering lakes, county fairs, music festivals, and campfire evenings under star-studded skies. Autumn paints Wisconsin in hues of gold, crimson, and orange, an artist's dream come alive, perfect for apple picking and scenic drives. As winter wraps Wisconsin in a sparkling blanket of snow, the state transforms into a playground for skiers, snowboarders, and ice fishing enthusiasts.

This guide aims to take you off the beaten path, revealing Wisconsin's hidden gems, local favorites, and iconic landmarks. Whether you're an urban explorer or nature enthusiast, history buff, foodie, or simply an adventurer at heart, Wisconsin's Best offers a day-by-day itinerary, each promising a unique experience.

Cheesehead Origins!

Residents of Wisconsin are often called "Cheeseheads." The term "cheesehead" began as an insult from German soldiers during World War II but is now worn as a badge of pride in Wisconsin.

From the historic lighthouses of Door County, the ethereal beauty of the Apostle Islands, the vibrant arts scene in Madison, the brewing traditions of Milwaukee, to the Native

American heritage at the effigy mounds - this book unravels Wisconsin's tapestry in all its colorful threads.

In this 2025-2026 edition, we've ensured that the experiences reflect the current times, keeping in mind the recent changes and trends, and highlighting destinations that promote sustainability and local culture. This is more than just a travel guide; it's a comprehensive, year-round exploration of a state that effortlessly marries tradition with innovation, nature with urban comfort, and simplicity with sophistication.

Welcome to the essence of the Midwest. Welcome to Wisconsin, where every day promises a unique adventure. Let's get started on this incredible 365-day journey through the Badger State. Enjoy the ride!

Chapter 2

How to Use This Guide

As you dive into this comprehensive guide, it's essential to understand its layout and functionalities. 'Wisconsin's Best: 365 Unique Adventures' has been designed for maximum user-friendly navigation, allowing you to seamlessly plan and customize your Wisconsin experience.

The Structure

This guidebook is organized into 365 unique adventures, one for each day of the year, but that doesn't mean you have to visit Wisconsin for a whole year to benefit from it.

How to Navigate the Adventures

Although the adventures are arranged in a specific order, this is a flexible guide. You're encouraged to skip around and choose your adventures based on your personal interests, time frame, and geographical location. An extensive index at the back of the book makes it easy to find adventures by name, region, or theme.

Personalizing Your Journey

We understand that every traveler has unique preferences. Some crave outdoor activities, others are drawn to historical sites, while many relish in food and wine escapades. Use the 'Theme' key at the start of the book to identify adventures that match your interests. Remember, it's your journey. Feel free to mix and match, slow down, or spice things up as you please.

Sharing the Journey

One of the joys of travel is sharing your experiences, whether with a travel companion or with friends and family back home. Remember to use the hashtag #JackAndKitty to connect with a community of fellow Wisconsin adventurers and possibly get featured on our social media platforms.

We hope 'Wisconsin's Best: 365 Unique Adventures' provides a memorable and smooth exploration of the diverse and beautiful state that is Wisconsin. Here's to discovering and enjoying your unique adventures in the Badger State.

For More Travel Tips Visit Our Blog

For even more helpful suggestions, be sure to visit our travel blog at **JackAndKitty.com** - here you'll find daily inspiration for having fun on your next trip to Wisconsin, the Midwest, and beyond!

Also, be sure to Subscribe to our YouTube channel for tons of videos to help you make the most out of your time in Wisconsin. In our video tours, we explore hidden gems, tips and tricks only the locals know about...and so much more! Here's the address you need to know: **https://www. youtube.com/@JackAndKitty**

Wanna Contact Us?

If you'd like to reach out to us, please email: **hello@ jackandkitty.com** - we'd love to hear from you. We hope you have an awesome trip!

Now, let's embark on this incredible journey together and create unforgettable stories in Wisconsin's captivating landscape.

Chapter 3

Travel Basics

With its unique mix of urban sophistication and rural charm, Wisconsin promises a diverse travel experience. Before setting off on your adventure, it's worth getting acquainted with some basics about the state. Let's dive into the details.

Geography and Climate

Situated in the Great Lakes region of the North Central United States, Wisconsin's geography ranges from the rugged ridges of the Driftless Area to the flat farmland of the Central Plain, from the dense forests of the Northwoods to the sandy beaches of its two Great Lakes, Michigan and Superior.

Climate-wise, Wisconsin enjoys all four seasons in their full glory. Summers (June to August) are generally warm and humid with temperatures ranging from 70 to 90°F. Winters (December to February) can be quite cold, with temperatures often dropping below freezing, and abundant snowfall transforming the state into a winter wonderland. Spring and autumn are mild and beautifully scenic, making them ideal for outdoor exploration.

When to Visit

The best time to visit Wisconsin truly depends on your interests. For outdoor activities such as hiking, biking, and camping, late spring to early fall (May to October) is most ideal. Winter sports enthusiasts should plan their visit during the snowy months of December through February. Autumn, particularly October, offers stunning fall foliage, especially in the northern and central parts of the state. Summer months bring numerous festivals and events, making them a lively time to explore Wisconsin's culture and traditions.

Getting to Wisconsin

Wisconsin is well-connected to the rest of the United States and the world. Major airports include General Mitchell International Airport in Milwaukee and Dane County Regional Airport in Madison. There are also several smaller regional airports throughout the state. By road, Wisconsin is accessible via numerous interstate highways. Amtrak provides rail service connecting Wisconsin to major cities in the Midwest.

Wisconsin's Within Reach!

Almost 1/3 of all Americans live within a 500-mile radius of Wisconsin, making it a central hub for millions. Another fun fact? Wisconsin has more water than any state except Alaska, Florida, and Michigan!

Getting Around Wisconsin

Public transportation is available in larger cities like Milwaukee and Madison, but if you're planning to explore extensively, renting a car is the best option. Wisconsin has a well-maintained network of state and interstate highways that make road trips a pleasure. For short distances within cities or towns, biking is a popular choice due to the state's extensive bicycle-friendly trails.

Currency

The official currency of Wisconsin, like the rest of the United States, is the US Dollar (USD). Credit and debit cards are widely accepted, and ATMs are easily found throughout the state. It's recommended to carry some cash for small businesses and rural areas where card machines might not be available.

Etiquette and Customs

Wisconsin is known for its friendly locals and Midwest hospitality. A few simple etiquette rules:

•Tipping: Standard practice is to tip 15-20% for good service in restaurants, bars, and taxis.

•Punctuality: Being on time is valued.

•Respect for Nature: Wisconsinites love their beautiful state and take conservation seriously. Follow all posted guidelines when visiting parks, trails, and natural areas.

Emergency Services

In case of an emergency, dial 911 for immediate assistance. It's recommended to have travel insurance that covers medical expenses. Major cities have well-equipped hospitals, and urgent care clinics are found even in smaller towns.

With these basics in mind, you are well-prepared to start your Wisconsin adventure. So pack your bags, get ready to explore, and remember – in the Badger State, every day promises a unique experience.

Chapter 4

Essential Adventures

In Wisconsin, there is a delightful surprise waiting at every corner. With each of its unique adventures revealing a different facet of the state's character, we have shortlisted twenty essential experiences that are particularly notable for their cultural, historical, or natural significance. These are the experiences you simply cannot miss. Dive into Wisconsin's heart and soul through these unforgettable adventures.

Adventure 1: Climb the Historic Lighthouses of Door County

Wisconsin's maritime heritage comes alive in the iconic lighthouses that dot the Door County shoreline. These century-old guardians offer incredible views of Lake Michigan and tell fascinating stories of the area's seafaring history. The Cana Island Lighthouse (8800 E Cana Island Rd, Baileys Harbor, WI 54202), in particular, is one of Wisconsin's most celebrated landmarks and offers a delightful adventure of climbing up its 97 steps to enjoy a spectacular panoramic view.

Adventure 2: Explore the Milwaukee Art Museum

This museum is not just about the art – it's an architectural marvel in its own right. With over 30,000 works of art, the museum hosts one of the largest collections in the country. Whether it's the Quadracci Pavilion, designed by the legendary Santiago Calatrava, or the postmodernist Kahler Building, the Milwaukee Art Museum (700 N Art Museum Dr, Milwaukee, WI 53202) is as much a visual treat on the outside as it is on the inside.

Adventure 3: Kayak the Apostle Islands Sea Caves

These mesmerizing sea caves on Lake Superior's shore are a testament to the power of nature. Paddle at your own pace through the pristine turquoise waters, as you discover the spectacular rock formations, echoing caverns, and hidden nooks. Each cave has its unique formations and colors, making for an unforgettable adventure.

Adventure 4: Experience the Green Bay Packers at Lambeau Field

Feel the pulse of Wisconsin's sports spirit at a Green Bay Packers game. Lambeau Field (1265 Lombardi Ave, Green Bay, WI 54304) is more than just a stadium; it's a place of community, camaraderie, and thrilling football. Join the fans, or "cheeseheads," as they are fondly known, in cheering on this legendary team, and experience the electrifying atmosphere of a live NFL game.

Adventure 5: Tour the State Capitol in Madison

Standing majestically at the heart of Madison, the Wisconsin State Capitol (2 E Main St, Madison, WI 53703) is an architectural delight. Embark on a guided tour to learn about its history and admire its Beaux-Arts architecture. Don't forget to visit the observation deck for a beautiful view of Madison's skyline and its surrounding lakes.

Adventure 6: Bike the Elroy-Sparta State Trail

Experience the great outdoors on this 32-mile bike trail, the first Rails-to-Trails project in the country. You'll pass through three rock tunnels and across idyllic farmlands and small towns. Along the way, interpretive signs tell the story of the area's natural and human history.

Adventure 7: Savor Wisconsin's Cheese Heritage

Wisconsin's cheese-making heritage is a story of tradition, innovation, and passion. A tour of a local cheese factory, such as the Henning's Wisconsin Cheese factory (20201 Point Creek Rd, Kiel, WI 53042), offers an in-depth look at the craft. From watching cheese curds being made to tasting a wide variety of cheeses, it's a gastronomic adventure not to be missed.

Adventure 8: Visit the House on the Rock

This is a place where reality and fantasy blend in a fascinating display of eclectic collections. Wander through rooms filled with antique dolls, the world's largest carousel, a giant sea creature, and countless other curiosities. The unique architecture of the house, built atop a rock chimney, adds to the sense of wonder and intrigue. The House on the Rock is located at: 5754 WI-23, Spring Green, WI 53588.

Adventure 9: Stroll Through Olbrich Botanical Gardens

These enchanting gardens, spanning 16 acres, are a haven for plant and nature lovers. From the fragrant Rose Garden to the serene Thai Garden, complete with an authentic Thai Pavilion, there's a world of natural beauty to explore at Olbrich Botanical Gardens (3330 Atwood Ave, Madison, WI 53704). Don't miss the tropical Bolz Conservatory, home to exotic plants, free-flying birds, and a waterfall.

Adventure 10: Experience the Wisconsin State Fair

A beloved tradition since 1851, the State Fair is a celebration of all things Wisconsin. The 11-day event is filled with live-stock exhibitions, arts and crafts displays, live music, carnival rides, and delicious food. The fair's famous cream puffs are a must-try treat.

Roll Out the Barrel!

Milwaukee, Wisconsin, has the highest rate of alcohol consumption in the United States. Milwaukee also hosts the world's largest music festival, Summerfest, which draws over 800,000 attendees annually!

Adventure 11: Roam Frank Lloyd Wright's Taliesin Estate

Nestled in the lush Wisconsin River valley, Taliesin was the beloved home and design laboratory of Frank Lloyd Wright, America's most famous architect. The guided tours offer an intimate look at Wright's personal life and architectural philosophy, and the estate's breathtaking landscapes inspire as much awe as the buildings themselves. Taliesin is located at: 5481 County Rd C, Spring Green, WI 53588.

Adventure 12: Delve into History at Old World Wisconsin

This open-air museum brings Wisconsin's immigrant past to life with a captivating display of historic buildings and live reenactments. Learn about the traditions and lifestyles of the state's early European settlers as you wander through the Norwegian farmstead, the German area, or the Crossroads Village. Old World Wisconsin is located at: W372 S9727 WI-67, Eagle, WI 53119.

Adventure 13: Indulge in a Fish Boil in Door County

A culinary tradition that dates back to the area's Scandinavian settlers, a Door County fish boil is not just a meal but an experience. Watch as the master boiler cooks locally-caught whitefish and potatoes in a pot over an open fire, and the dramatic "boil-over" that signifies the end of cooking. The meal, often accompanied by stories and music, is a taste of Wisconsin's cultural heritage.

Adventure 14: Catch a Performance at the American Players Theatre

Nestled in a wooded hillside, the American Players Theatre (5950 Golf Course Rd, Spring Green, WI 53588) offers a unique theater experience. Their outdoor stage under the stars makes watching the performances, ranging from Shakespeare to modern classics, a magical experience. With the sounds of nature as the backdrop, it's a celebration of art in its most natural form.

Adventure 15: Enjoy Beer Sampling in Milwaukee

Known as "Brew City," Milwaukee has a rich brewing heritage that goes back to its early German settlers. Visit one of the historic breweries for a taste of this tradition, or explore the city's vibrant craft beer scene at a modern microbrewery. Beer tours offer a behind-the-scenes look at the brewing process and, of course, plenty of samples to enjoy.

Adventure 16: Hike in Devil's Lake State Park

Devil's Lake State Park (S5975 Park Rd, Baraboo, WI 53913) is a paradise for outdoor enthusiasts. The park's hiking trails offer a range of difficulties, from leisurely lakeside strolls to challenging climbs. The Balanced Rock Trail and the Ice Age National Scenic Trail are particularly popular, offering stunning views of the lake and the unique rock formations that gave the park its name.

Adventure 17: Discover Native American Heritage at the Effigy Mounds

These ancient earthworks, built by the indigenous peoples of Wisconsin, are sacred sites and intriguing glimpses into the state's pre-European history. Located near the Mississippi River, the mounds are shaped like animals and other symbols. The interpretive center offers insights into the mound builders' cultures and beliefs. Effigy Mound Preserve is located at: Indian Mound Pkwy, Whitewater, WI 53190.

Adventure 18: Ski at Granite Peak

With 75 runs, this ski resort offers a variety of slopes for all skill levels. Whether you're a seasoned skier or a beginner taking your first lesson, Granite Peak Ski Area (227200 Snowbird Ave, Wausau, WI 54401) promises a fun-filled day of winter sports. Enjoy the thrill of downhill skiing or snowboarding amidst the stunning natural beauty of the Rib Mountain State Park (149801 State Park Rd, Wausau, WI 54401).

Adventure 19: Wander Through the Milwaukee Public Market

This bustling market in the historic Third Ward district is a food lover's paradise. Fresh produce, locally-sourced meats, gourmet cheese, artisanal chocolates, and more—there's something to delight every palate. Taste your way through different cuisines, from seafood to Italian to Middle Eastern, or pick up some local products to cook your own Wisconsin-inspired meal. The Milwaukee Public Market is located at: 400 N Water St, Milwaukee, WI 53202.

Adventure 20: Cruise the Wisconsin River on a Dells Boat Tour

Experience the natural beauty of the Wisconsin Dells with a scenic boat tour. Marvel at the towering sandstone cliffs that line the river, carved by glaciers thousands of years ago. Spot wildlife along the shores, learn about the area's unique geology from your guide, and soak in the peaceful ambience of this unspoiled wilderness.

Chapter 5

Cultural Adventures

For the curious traveler, Wisconsin's diverse cultural scene offers an exciting array of experiences that connect you to the heart of this vibrant state. Uncover the rich history, taste the delectable local foods, revel in the thriving arts scene, and immerse yourself in the state's traditions. These cultural adventures reveal the stories that make Wisconsin unique.

Adventure 21: Attend a Summerfest Concert in Milwaukee

As one of the world's largest music festivals, Summerfest in Milwaukee brings together music lovers from all corners of the globe. With 11 days of performances by top artists spanning various genres, there's a concert for every music taste. Aside from the music, the festival also offers comedy acts, family activities, and mouth-watering food from local vendors. Each Summerfest experience is a celebration of music, community, and the vibrant energy of Milwaukee's cultural scene.

Adventure 22: Visit Circus World in Baraboo

Dive into Wisconsin's circus history at Circus World (550 Water St, Baraboo, WI 53913), the original winter quarters of the Ringling Bros. Circus. Here, history comes alive with vintage circus posters, an impressive collection of antique circus wagons, and live performances in the Hippodrome. Watch acrobats and jugglers perform thrilling stunts, be charmed by the magic shows, and enjoy the laughter and awe-inspiring performances that continue the rich tradition of the American circus.

Adventure 23: Explore the Harley-Davidson Museum in Milwaukee

The Harley-Davidson Museum (400 W Canal St, Milwaukee, WI 53201) is a must-visit for motorcycle enthusiasts and anyone with an interest in American history. More than a motorcycle museum, this is a testament to over 100 years of history, culture, and the pursuit of freedom. See the earliest Harley "Serial Number One," take a faux ride through the factory, and marvel at the powerful bikes from different eras.

Adventure 24: Wander the Streets of Cedarburg's Historic Downtown

Cedarburg's Historic Downtown is a charming window into the past, with its well-preserved 19th-century buildings, vintage inns, and old-fashioned candy shops. Spend a leisurely day browsing the unique boutiques and galleries, savoring the homemade ice cream, and soaking up the town's quaint, historic ambiance.

Adventure 25: Experience the Ojibwe Powwow

Experience Native American culture firsthand at the Ojibwe Powwow, where tribal members gather to celebrate their traditions through music, dance, and communal feasting. Watch the mesmerizing dances, each with its own symbolic meaning, listen to the powerful beat of the drum, and taste traditional Ojibwe foods. The Powwow is an opportunity to learn about and respect the rich heritage of Wisconsin's indigenous people.

Adventure 26: Discover Pabst Mansion in Milwaukee

Explore the opulence of the Gilded Age at the Pabst Mansion (2000 W Wisconsin Ave, Milwaukee, WI 53233), the former home of beer magnate Captain Frederick Pabst. The mansion's stunning architecture, beautifully restored interiors, and intricate decorations offer a glimpse into the life of one of Milwaukee's most influential families. The collection of original furnishings, art, and personal items add an intimate touch to the grandeur.

Adventure 27: Delight in the Polka Music Scene

Polka music, with its lively rhythms and joyful dance steps, is an integral part of Wisconsin's cultural fabric. Attend a polka festival, such as the Pulaski Polka Days or the Wisconsin State Polka Festival, or dance the night away at a local polka club. Whether you're a seasoned polka dancer or trying it for the first time, the vibrant polka scene is a delightful cultural experience.

Adventure 28: Explore The National Railroad Museum in Green Bay

The National Railroad Museum (2285 S Broadway, Ashwaubenon, WI 54304) takes you on a fascinating journey through the history of American railroads. Stand in awe of the enormous locomotives, climb aboard historical cars, and learn about the role of railroads in shaping the nation. The Dwight D. Eisenhower, a British locomotive that transported the Supreme Commander during World War II, is one of the museum's highlights.

Adventure 29: Wisconsin's Vibrant Cultural Scene...Under the Big Top

Immerse yourself in Wisconsin's vibrant cultural scene at Big Top Chautauqua (32525 Ski Hill Rd, Bayfield, WI 54814). Home to a one-of-a-kind canvas theatre tent, this venue brings history, arts, and community together through eclectic performances. The Big Top presents a wide variety of high-quality events, from concerts to theatre productions, featuring both local talent and international artists. Experience the joy of live performance under a star-studded sky, capturing the true essence of Wisconsin's lively and diverse cultural tapestry.

Adventure 30: Visit the Kohler Design Center

A mecca for design enthusiasts, the Kohler Design Center (101 Upper Rd, Kohler, WI 53044) showcases the innovative designs of the Kohler Company. Wander through the three-level showroom filled with the latest in kitchen and bath products, marvel at the historic displays, and take a peek into the craftsmanship that goes into each product in the factory tour.

They See Me Trollin'

Mount Horeb, Wisconsin, is renowned as the "Troll Capital of the World." To celebrate its rich Norwegian heritage, the town has installed numerous troll carvings to attract tourists.

Adventure 31: Tour Ten Chimneys in Genesee Depot

Once the summer retreat of Broadway legends Alfred Lunt and Lynn Fontanne, Ten Chimneys (S43 W31575 Depot Rd, Waukesha, WI 53189) is a testament to the glamour of the theatrical world. The estate is filled with original furnishings, art collections, and personal mementos, each telling a story about the couple's life and their illustrious guests. The beautifully landscaped gardens add to the charm of the estate.

Adventure 32: Discover the Heritage Hill State Historical Park in Green Bay

Step back in time at the Heritage Hill State Historical Park (2640 S Webster Ave, Green Bay, WI 54301), a 48-acre outdoor museum that celebrates Northeast Wisconsin's rich heritage. The park features over 25 historic buildings and structures, from a fur trade cabin to a Belgian farmhouse, each filled with period furnishings and brought to life by costumed interpreters.

Adventure 33: Indulge in the Friday Night Fish Fry Tradition

The Friday Night Fish Fry is a beloved Wisconsin tradition, one that brings together communities in local taverns and family-run supper clubs. Indulge in a platter of crispy, beer-battered fish (usually perch, walleye, or cod), served with coleslaw, rye bread, and a generous helping of tartar sauce. The convivial atmosphere, hearty food, and live polka music make it a truly Wisconsinite experience.

Adventure 34: Stroll the Riverwalk in Milwaukee

The Riverwalk in Milwaukee is a vibrant hub of art, dining, and entertainment. As you stroll along the beautifully landscaped paths, you'll come across art installations, historic architecture, and bustling breweries. The Riverwalk is also home to the iconic Bronze Fonz statue (N Riverwalk Way, Milwaukee, WI 53202), a tribute to the popular television show "Happy Days."

Adventure 35: Learn at the EAA AirVenture Museum in Oshkosh

At the EAA AirVenture Museum (3000 Poberezny Rd, Oshkosh, WI 54902), immerse yourself in the world of aviation and its history. The museum features more than 200 aircraft, from antiques and classics to warbirds and home-built aircraft. During the annual EAA AirVenture Oshkosh event, you can witness exciting air shows, meet aviation pioneers, and even get a chance to fly in some historic aircraft.

Adventure 36: Enjoy a Performance at the Milwaukee Symphony Orchestra

Treat your ears to a performance by the Milwaukee Symphony Orchestra, one of the country's top orchestras. The ensemble's concerts, ranging from classical to pop, are renowned for their artistic excellence. The Orchestra's grand new home, the Bradley Symphony Center (212 W Wisconsin Ave, Milwaukee, WI 53203), is a stunningly restored historic theater that adds to the magic of the musical experience.

Adventure 37: Savor Wisconsin's Dairy Delights

Wisconsin is America's Dairyland, and no trip would be complete without sampling its dairy delights. Visit a local dairy farm or creamery, such as the Clock Shadow Creamery (138 W Bruce St, Milwaukee, WI 53204), to see how Wisconsin's famous cheeses are made, and, of course, to taste the fresh, creamy products. And don't forget to try the state's legendary custard-style ice cream!

Adventure 38: Experience Hmong Culture at the Hmong New Year Celebration

Experience the vibrant Hmong culture at the Hmong New Year celebration in Milwaukee. This cultural event features colorful traditional costumes, music, dance, and sports competitions, along with Hmong cuisine and crafts. It's a wonderful way to learn about the rich traditions of the Hmong community, one of Wisconsin's largest Asian communities.

Adventure 39: Explore the Vibrant Madison's Farmers Market

Widely known as one of America's best farmers' markets, Madison's Dane County Farmers Market (2 E Main St, Madison, WI 53703) provides a feast for the senses. With more than 150 vendors, it's the perfect place to sample

Wisconsin's cheese, taste freshly picked fruits, and savor mouthwatering pastries. The market also features an array of beautifully crafted handmade items, from jewelry to pottery.

Adventure 40: Dive into Frank Lloyd Wright's Legacy in Racine

In Racine, you can visit the SC Johnson corporate headquarters (1525 Howe St, Racine, WI 53403), one of Frank Lloyd Wright's architectural masterpieces. The Administration Building, with its unique dendriform columns, and the Research Tower, are testaments to Wright's innovative designs. A visit to Wingspread, a Wright-designed residence, completes the experience.

Adventure 41: Visit the Basilica of St. Josaphat in Milwaukee

Marvel at the grandeur of the Basilica of St. Josaphat (2333 S 6th St, Milwaukee, WI 53215), one of the largest basilicas in the country. Built in the Roman Renaissance style, the basilica's stunning architecture, intricate mosaics, and breathtaking paintings offer a tranquil and inspiring visit.

Adventure 42: Enjoy the Sheboygan Bratwurst Days

Get a taste of Sheboygan at the Bratwurst Days, a festival that celebrates the city's bratwurst-making tradition. Enjoy the Bratwurst Eating contest, the Brat Trot run, and the infamous Johnsonville World Bratwurst Eating Championship.

Of course, there's plenty of bratwurst to enjoy, along with music, fun, and camaraderie.

Adventure 43: Step into the Swiss Heritage at New Glarus

Immerse yourself in Swiss heritage in the charming town of New Glarus. Known as "America's Little Switzerland," the town features Swiss-style architecture, a Swiss Historical Village Musuem (612 7th Ave, New Glarus, WI 53574), and the annual Wilhelm Tell Festival, which presents a Swiss folklore play. Don't miss the chance to sample Swiss delicacies and locally-brewed Swiss beer.

Chapter 6

Adventures for Families with Kids

Wisconsin is a wonderland for families, with a wealth of attractions that will delight kids and adults alike. Whether your family loves the great outdoors, historical sites, sports, or interactive learning experiences, Wisconsin has an adventure that will create lasting memories. Each of these family-friendly adventures is designed to be both fun and educational, providing experiences that will broaden horizons and deepen family bonds.

Adventure 44: Explore the Children's Museum of Eau Claire

The Children's Museum of Eau Claire (126 N Barstow St, Eau Claire, WI 54703) is a fantastic space where kids can learn through play. The interactive exhibits stimulate curiosity and encourage kids to explore the world around them. From the 'Bitty City' designed to teach social skills to the 'Water Works' exhibit that introduces the principles of fluid dynamics, there's an educational adventure around every corner.

Adventure 45: Visit the Henry Vilas Zoo in Madison

The Henry Vilas Zoo (702 S Randall Ave, Madison, WI 53715) is a treat for animal lovers of all ages. The zoo features an array of exotic animals from around the world, including polar bears, lions, and giraffes. With free admission, the zoo is committed to providing access to nature and wildlife education for everyone.

Adventure 46: Learn at the Discovery World Science and Technology Museum in Milwaukee

Discovery World (500 N Harbor Dr, Milwaukee, WI 53202) is a treasure trove of interactive science and technology exhibits. Children can learn about the Great Lakes ecosystem, experience the principles of physics in action, or explore the intricacies of human anatomy. The museum's Reiman Aquarium is also a huge hit with kids, where they can touch stingrays and view colorful sea creatures.

Adventure 47: Have Fun at the Bay Beach Amusement Park in Green Bay

Bay Beach Amusement Park (1313 Bay Beach Rd, Green Bay, WI 54302) is a nostalgic treat with its vintage rides and old-school charm. Whether it's riding the Zippin Pippin roller coaster, enjoying the view from the Ferris wheel, or playing in the park's expansive green spaces, there's something for everyone. It's a fun-filled outing that's easy on the wallet.

Adventure 48: Marvel at the Cave of the Mounds in Blue Mounds

The Cave of the Mounds (2975 Cave of the Mounds Rd, Blue Mounds, WI 53517), a National Natural Landmark, is a subterranean wonderland of beautiful stalactites and stalagmites. Kids will be awestruck as they journey through the cave's illuminated paths, learning about geology and the fascinating formations created over thousands of years.

Adventure 49: Visit the Milwaukee County Zoo

Spanning over 200 acres, the Milwaukee County Zoo (10001 W Bluemound Rd, Milwaukee, WI 53226) is home to over 2,000 animals. Families can see everything from African elephants to Arctic polar bears, ride the Safari Train, and interact with farm animals at the Family Farm. The zoo's commitment to animal conservation makes it a fun and educational outing.

Adventure 50: Unleash Creativity at the Art Garage in Green Bay

At the Art Garage (1400 Cedar St, Green Bay, WI 54302), children can discover their artistic talents through a variety of workshops and classes. From painting and drawing to sculpture and crafts, the Art Garage nurtures creativity and expression. The monthly 'Family Fun Day' offers a range of art projects suitable for all ages.

Adventure 51: Experience the International Crane Foundation in Baraboo

Home to all 15 species of cranes in the world, the International Crane Foundation (E11376 Shady Lane Rd, Baraboo, WI 53913) offers a unique opportunity to learn about these majestic birds and the efforts to preserve them. Kids can take part in interactive displays, watch cranes in their naturalistic habitats, and learn about the importance of biodiversity.

Adventure 52: Wander through the Milwaukee Public Museum

The Milwaukee Public Museum (800 W Wells St, Milwaukee, WI 53233) provides an immersive learning experience with its lifelike dioramas and interactive exhibits. Families can walk through a recreation of old Milwaukee, stand beneath a life-sized T-Rex, or explore the butterfly garden. The planetarium offers spectacular celestial shows that will captivate children and adults alike.

Adventure 53: Spend a Day at Noah's Ark Water Park in Wisconsin Dells

Noah's Ark Water Park (1410 Wisconsin Dells Pkwy, Wisconsin Dells, WI 53965), the largest water park in America, guarantees a day full of splashy fun. With numerous water slides, wave pools, lazy rivers, and a 4-D

Dive-In Theater, there are activities to suit every age and thrill level. The park is also committed to safety, ensuring a fun and secure environment for families.

Barbie's a Cheesehead!

In the world of Barbie, the iconic doll hails from the fictional town of Willows, Wisconsin.

Adventure 54: Discover Nature at the Urban Ecology Center in Milwaukee

The Urban Ecology Center (1859 N 40th St, Milwaukee, WI 53208) provides families with the opportunity to connect with nature right in the city. With its trails, gardens, and playground, children can explore the outdoors, learn about ecosystems, and engage in hands-on environmental education. It's a green oasis in the urban landscape.

Adventure 55: Visit Lambeau Field for a Packers Family Night

Packers Family Night at Lambeau Field (1265 Lombardi Ave, Green Bay, WI 54304) is a wonderful introduction to football for young fans. The evening features a practice game, fireworks, and activities for kids. Even if you're not football enthusiasts, the energy and community spirit make it a memorable experience.

Adventure 56: Take a Horse-Drawn Sleigh Ride at Palmquist Farm

At Palmquist Farm (N5136 River Rd, Brantwood, WI 54513), families can enjoy a relaxing horse-drawn sleigh ride through the scenic countryside. They've been around since 1949! It's a delightful way to take in the rural beauty of Wisconsin and create a new tradition. Plus, kids will love the opportunity to meet the friendly horses!

Adventure 57: Explore the Northwoods Wildlife Center in Minocqua

At the Northwoods Wildlife Center (8683 S Blumenstein Rd, Minocqua, WI 54548), families can learn about Wisconsin's native wildlife, from owls and eagles to turtles and otters. The center rehabilitates injured animals, and their guided tours offer a closer look at these creatures while learning about the importance of wildlife conservation.

Adventure 58: Enjoy the Outdoors at High Cliff State Park

High Cliff State Park (N7630 State Park Rd, Sherwood, WI 54169) offers families a chance to enjoy Wisconsin's natural beauty. Whether it's hiking along the scenic trails, swimming in Lake Winnebago, or exploring the park's unique geological features, there are plenty of outdoor activities to keep the whole family entertained.

Adventure 59: Visit the Betty Brinn Children's Museum in Milwaukee

At the Betty Brinn Children's Museum (929 E Wisconsin Ave, Milwaukee, WI 53202), kids can learn through hands-on play. The museum features interactive exhibits that encourage kids to explore the world around them, from a pretend city where they can learn about different professions to a 'Tot Spot' designed for toddlers.

Adventure 60: Learn History at the Wisconsin Veterans Museum

The Wisconsin Veterans Museum (30 W Mifflin St, Madison, WI 53703) offers families a meaningful way to learn about the state's military history. Through personal stories and artifacts, the museum highlights the experiences of Wisconsin's military men and women from the Civil War to the present.

Adventure 61: Enjoy Outdoor Activities at the Blue Mound State Park

Blue Mound State Park (4350 Mounds Park Rd, Blue Mounds, WI 53517) is a great destination for families who love outdoor activities. You can go hiking, biking, camping, or swimming in the park's pool. In winter, the park offers cross-country skiing and snowshoeing. The park's observation towers also provide panoramic views of the surrounding area.

Adventure 62: Explore the Wisconsin Maritime Museum

At the Wisconsin Maritime Museum (75 Maritime Dr, Manitowoc, WI 54220), families can learn about the state's rich maritime history. The museum features interactive exhibits, a children's waterway room, and the chance to tour the USS Cobia, a World War II submarine.

Adventure 63: Family Fun at Wisconsin Dells

Often touted as the "Waterpark Capital of the World," Wisconsin Dells is a family favorite and a must-visit for those seeking thrills and spills. This lively city offers an array of water-based attractions, including Noah's Ark, the largest water park in America, and Kalahari, an African-themed indoor waterpark resort. Apart from its famous waterparks, the Dells also provides fun outdoor activities like zip-lining, golf, and scenic boat tours. From water slides to wave pools and everything in between, Wisconsin Dells is an unmatched destination for family-oriented fun in Wisconsin.

Adventure 64: Enjoy a Day at the Racine Zoo

Located on the shores of Lake Michigan, the Racine Zoo (2131 N Main St, Racine, WI 53402) offers a wonderful day out for the whole family. The zoo is home to over 100 species of animals and offers various interactive experiences, including giraffe encounters and camel rides.

Adventure 65: Visit the Milwaukee Children's Choir

If your family enjoys music, a visit to a Milwaukee Children's Choir (427 E Stewart St #100, Milwaukee, WI 53207) performance is a must. These young singers will impress you with their talent and dedication, and the experience might even inspire your kids to get involved in music themselves.

Adventure 66: Embrace the Joy of Reading at Wisconsin's Public Libraries

In Wisconsin, summer isn't just about outdoor exploration; it's also about nurturing young minds with the gift of reading. Wisconsin's public libraries offer captivating summer reading programs aimed at encouraging kids to delve into the world of books, fostering a lifelong love for reading. These programs are a popular hit among families, as they provide an exciting alternative to screen time, incorporate fun, interactive activities, and keep the young ones intellectually engaged during their break. So while you're adventuring in the Badger State, check out these programs; who knows, your child's fondest summer memory might be discovering their new favorite book!

Chapter 7

Urban Adventures

While Wisconsin's natural beauty is well known, the state's urban centers offer an array of their own unique adventures. From the vibrant arts scene to historical landmarks, engaging museums, and diverse culinary experiences, Wisconsin's cities are bursting with opportunities for exploration. This chapter presents urban adventures that will take you into the heart of Wisconsin's urban life, unveiling the culture, history, and vibrancy of its cities.

Adventure 67: Explore La Crosse's Historic Downtown

La Crosse's historic downtown is a delightful mix of historic buildings, boutique shops, and diverse eateries. Visitors can take a leisurely stroll along the streets, visit the local art galleries, and enjoy the architectural beauty of the well-preserved buildings.

Adventure 68: Attend a Show at The Rep in Milwaukee

Milwaukee Repertory Theater (108 E Wells St, Milwaukee, WI 53202), known as The Rep, is a cornerstone of Milwaukee's vibrant arts scene. With a lineup of shows that includes classic dramas, contemporary plays, and musicals, The Rep provides an enriching cultural experience.

Adventure 69: Dine at Sanford Restaurant in Milwaukee

Experience the culinary genius of James Beard Award-winning chef, Sanford D'Amato, at Sanford Restaurant (1547 N Jackson St, Milwaukee, WI 53202). This fine-dining establishment features a menu of innovative dishes using local, seasonal ingredients and offers an exceptional wine list.

Adventure 70: Tour the Allen-Bradley Clock Tower in Milwaukee

The Allen-Bradley Clock Tower (1201 S 2nd St, Milwaukee, WI 53204), also known as the Rockwell Automation Clock Tower, is an iconic part of Milwaukee's skyline. Taking a tour of the tower gives visitors a glimpse into the city's industrial history and a breathtaking view of the city from its observation deck.

Adventure 71: Visit Kenosha's Public Museums

Kenosha's public museums offer a variety of cultural experiences. The Kenosha Public Museum (5500 1st Ave, Kenosha, WI 53140) features exhibits on natural sciences and fine arts, the Civil War Museum (5400 1st Ave, Kenosha, WI 53140) provides a deep dive into the history of the Civil War, and the Dinosaur Discovery Museum (5608 10th Ave, Kenosha, WI 53140) is a hit with kids and adults alike.

Adventure 72: Explore Beloit's Downtown Art Scene

Beloit's downtown area is an art lover's dream with its collection of public art installations, including murals, sculptures, and art galleries. The Beloit Artwalk is a self-guided tour that takes visitors through these art installations, each telling a unique story about the city and its culture.

Adventure 73: Visit the East Side Business District in Milwaukee

The East Side Business District in Milwaukee offers an eclectic mix of shops, restaurants, and entertainment venues. From vintage clothing stores to artisanal cheese shops, visitors can find a variety of unique shopping experiences.

Adventure 74: Attend a Concert at the Pabst Theater in Milwaukee

Built in 1895, the Pabst Theater (144 E Wells St, Milwaukee, WI 53202) is a historic venue that hosts a variety of concerts, plays, and comedy shows. It's not just the performances that are worth seeing—the theater itself, with its beautiful baroque interior, is a sight to behold.

Adventure 75: Explore the Urban Ecology Center's Three Branches in Milwaukee

The Urban Ecology Center has three branches in Milwaukee, each offering unique opportunities to learn about urban ecology. Visitors can explore native plant gardens, check out the green building designs, or join guided walks and workshops.

Adventure 76: Attend the La Crosse Oktoberfest

La Crosse Oktoberfest is a week-long celebration of German culture. Visitors can enjoy traditional German music, food, and, of course, beer. The event also includes a parade, a craft beer night, and various competitions.

A Ghostly Record!

Wisconsin reportedly has more ghosts per square mile than any other state. Spooky and fascinating!

Adventure 77: Visit America's Black Holocaust Museum

America's Black Holocaust Museum (401 W North Ave, Milwaukee, WI 53212) explores the history and enduring legacy of the African diaspora, particularly focusing on the black experience in America. Visitors can learn about the injustices faced by the black community, their resilience, and contributions to society.

Adventure 78: Stroll along the Riverwalk in Sheboygan

The Riverwalk in Sheboygan provides a relaxing urban adventure. The trail winds along the Sheboygan River, passing through the city's downtown, where visitors can take in the sights, stop by local shops, or enjoy a meal at a riverside restaurant.

Adventure 79: Tour the Tenuta's Delicatessen in Kenosha

Tenuta's Delicatessen (3203 52nd St, Kenosha, WI 53144) is a culinary landmark. This Italian grocery store offers a variety of Italian and specialty foods, including handmade sausages, gourmet cheeses, and homemade pasta. Visitors can tour the store, taste the products, and even take a cooking class.

Adventure 80: Visit the Madison Museum of Contemporary Art

The Madison Museum of Contemporary Art (227 State St, Madison, WI 53703) features a collection of modern and contemporary art, including paintings, sculptures, and photographs. The museum also hosts a variety of temporary exhibitions and events, offering visitors a unique insight into the contemporary art scene.

Adventure 81: Explore the Historic Third Ward in Milwaukee

The Historic Third Ward in Milwaukee is a vibrant neighborhood known for its art galleries, boutiques, and eateries. Visitors can explore the Milwaukee Public Market (400 N Water St, Milwaukee, WI 53202), wander through art-filled streets during the quarterly Gallery Night and Day, or watch a performance at the Broadway Theatre Center (158 N Broadway, Milwaukee, WI 53202).

Adventure 82: Visit the Janesville Rotary Gardens

The Janesville Rotary Gardens (1455 Palmer Dr, Janesville, WI 53545) are a testament to the transformative power of a dedicated community. These internationally-themed botanical gardens feature 24 different garden styles on 20 acres, providing a serene urban escape.

Adventure 83: Explore the Mitchell Park Horticultural Conservatory in Milwaukee

Known as The Domes, the Mitchell Park Horticultural Conservatory (524 S Layton Blvd, Milwaukee, WI 53215) features three distinct climates - a desert, a tropical jungle, and a floral garden. Each dome provides a unique experience of plant life and is a wonderful urban adventure for all ages.

Adventure 84: Visit the SafeHouse Restaurant in Milwaukee

For a unique dining adventure, visit the SafeHouse Restaurant (779 N Front St, Milwaukee, WI 53202). This spy-themed restaurant requires a password for entry, offers secret-agent-inspired food and drinks, and is full of spy paraphernalia and secret passages.

Adventure 85: Take a Food Tour in Madison

Madison's culinary scene is diverse and vibrant. Taking a food tour offers visitors a chance to sample a variety of local flavors, from farm-to-table fare to international cuisine, all while learning about Madison's food culture and history.

Adventure 86: Attend a Show at the Majestic Theatre in Madison

The Majestic Theatre (115 King St, Madison, WI 53703) is the city's oldest theater and offers a variety of performances, including concerts, comedy shows, and film screenings. Its intimate setting provides a unique venue for enjoying live entertainment.

Adventure 87: Visit the Racine Art Museum

The Racine Art Museum (441 Main St, Racine, WI 53403) houses a contemporary craft collection, with more than 9,500 pieces in ceramics, fibers, glass, metals, and wood. It's a must-visit for art lovers and those interested in the intersection of craft, design, and fine art.

Adventure 88: Explore the Houdini Plaza in Appleton

Named after the famous magician who claimed Appleton as his hometown, Houdini Plaza (100 W Lawrence St, Appleton, WI 54911) is a public square that hosts various events throughout the year, including summer concerts and a weekly farmers market. The plaza also features a bust of Houdini himself, making for an intriguing urban exploration.

Adventure 89: Take a Tour of Milwaukee's Bronzeville District

Milwaukee's Bronzeville District was a thriving African American economic and social hub in the early 20th century. Today, the district is being revitalized and visitors can take a tour to learn about its rich history, visit art galleries, and enjoy local cuisine.

Chapter 8

Why Is Wisconsin Known For Cheese? You Asked, We Answered!

Back in the 1800s, Wisconsin was a popular spot for European immigrants to settle down and start farms. The state's cool climate and lush green pastures were perfect for raising happy, healthy cows. And you know what happy cows make? That's right – delicious milk!

As more and more farmers began producing milk, they needed a way to preserve it. That's when they started making cheese, and boy, did they get good at it!

Fast forward to today, and Wisconsin is home to over 1,200 licensed cheesemakers who create more than 600 different types of cheese. From classic cheddar to fancy artisanal varieties, these folks take their cheese seriously.

In fact, Wisconsin is the only state that requires its cheesemakers to have a license. To get one, they have to complete rigorous training and pass a test. It's like getting a degree in cheese!

When you visit Wisconsin, you'll quickly realize that cheese is a way of life. There are cheese festivals, cheese tours, and even a Cheese Castle (yes, really!). You can sample your way through cheese shops, indulge in cheesy dishes at local restaurants, and take home some tasty souvenirs.

One of the most famous Wisconsin cheese creations is the cheese curd. These little nuggets of goodness are made fresh daily and have a satisfying squeak when you bite into them. Trust us; they're addictive!

Wisconsin's perfect combination of climate, culture, and craftsmanship has made it a cheese lover's paradise. The state's dedication to quality and tradition has earned it a well-deserved reputation for producing some of the best cheese in the world.

Chapter 9

Nature and Wildlife Adventures

Wisconsin's diverse natural landscapes, from dense forests and tranquil lakes to rolling farmlands and towering bluffs, serve as a paradise for nature and wildlife enthusiasts. This chapter will guide you on exciting nature and wildlife adventures that will allow you to discover Wisconsin's ecological richness and abundant wildlife. Whether you are a birdwatcher, a hiker, a fishing enthusiast, or simply a nature lover, there is an adventure waiting for you.

Adventure 90: Birdwatching at the Horicon Marsh

Horicon Marsh is the largest freshwater cattail marsh in the United States and a globally important bird area. A paradise for birdwatchers, the marsh is home to over 300 bird species. Various trails and overlooks provide excellent birdwatching opportunities year-round.

Adventure 91: Explore Kettle Moraine State Forest

The Kettle Moraine State Forest offers a variety of nature-based activities. Hike the Ice Age Trail, explore glacial landforms, camp under the stars, or enjoy fishing and swimming in one of the many lakes and streams. The forest's diverse habitats support a rich array of wildlife, making it a fantastic location for nature photography.

Adventure 92: Canoeing in the Flambeau River State Forest

The Flambeau River State Forest offers some of Wisconsin's best canoeing experiences. Its two forks offer varying levels of difficulty and scenery, making it suitable for both beginner and experienced paddlers. You can also camp along the riverbank and enjoy the tranquility of the forest.

Adventure 93: Wildlife Spotting at Crex Meadows

Crex Meadows (102 Crex Ave, Grantsburg, WI 54840) is a wildlife area where visitors can spot various wildlife, including sandhill cranes, loons, and foxes. There are auto tour routes and trails for visitors, and interpretive programs are offered throughout the year.

Adventure 94: Wildlife Watcher's Quest

Embark on a Wildlife Watcher's Quest by creating a personalized checklist of native Wisconsin wildlife species. Armed with this checklist and a pair of binoculars, explore natural areas like national parks, wildlife refuges, and nature reserves. Keep a keen eye out for birds, mammals, reptiles, and amphibians, checking them off as you spot them. This engaging activity allows visitors to immerse themselves in Wisconsin's biodiversity, fostering a deeper appreciation for wildlife and the importance of conservation.

Adventure 95: Hike the St. Croix National Scenic Riverway

The St. Croix National Scenic Riverway offers excellent hiking opportunities. The Riverway's diverse habitats support a wide array of wildlife, from bald eagles to white-tailed deer. Whether you opt for a challenging hike or a leisurely walk, the scenic views of the river are sure to captivate you.

Adventure 96: Visit the Heckrodt Wetland Reserve in Menasha

The Heckrodt Wetland Reserve (1305 Plank Rd, Menasha, WI 54952) offers 3 miles of trails through woodland, wetland, and prairie habitats. The Reserve also has a Nature Center with interactive exhibits and seasonal programs. It's a great location for wildlife viewing, with frequent sightings of muskrats, turtles, and various bird species.

Adventure 97: Explore the Lakeshore Nature Preserve in Madison

The Lakeshore Nature Preserve (2000 University Bay Dr, Madison, WI 53705) protects rare habitats along the shores of Lake Mendota. Visitors can enjoy birdwatching, explore woodland trails, or simply relax by the lake. The Preserve is also an excellent location for wildlife photography.

Adventure 98: Hike the Ice Age National Scenic Trail

The Ice Age National Scenic Trail traverses some of Wisconsin's most beautiful landscapes shaped by the last Ice Age. The trail offers stunning views of glacial landforms, forests, and prairies, and provides excellent opportunities for birdwatching and wildlife viewing.

Adventure 99: Visit the Willow River State Park

Willow River State Park (1034 Co Hwy A, Hudson, WI 54016) offers a variety of recreational activities. Visitors can hike to the stunning Willow Falls, enjoy fishing or boating on Little Falls Lake, or explore the park's diverse habitats, which support a wide array of wildlife.

Flowing Against the Norm!

The Fox River is unique as it flows north, against the usual direction for rivers in the United States.

Adventure 100: Explore the North Country National Scenic Trail

The North Country National Scenic Trail, which spans several states, offers some of the best hiking experiences in Wisconsin. It takes hikers through a variety of landscapes, including forests, farmlands, and wetlands, and offers excellent opportunities for wildlife viewing.

Adventure 101: Visit the New Zoo & Adventure Park in Green Bay

The New Zoo & Adventure Park (4378 Reforestation Rd, Green Bay, WI 54313) offers an interactive wildlife experience. Visitors can get up close with animals from around the world, feed giraffes, and even ride a zip line. The park's focus on conservation and education makes it an excellent adventure for families.

Adventure 102: Explore the Richard Bong State Recreation Area

Richard Bong State Recreation Area (26313 Burlington Rd, Kansasville, WI 53139) offers diverse outdoor recreational opportunities. Visitors can explore prairies and wetlands, spot wildlife from observation towers, or engage in water activities on Wolf Lake.

Adventure 103: Birdwatching at the Ridges Sanctuary in Door County

The Ridges Sanctuary (8166 WI-57, Baileys Harbor, WI 54202) in Door County is Wisconsin's oldest private nature preserve. Known for its unique ridges and swales, it's a hotspot for birdwatching, with more than 200 bird species recorded.

Adventure 104: Hike the Chequamegon-Nicolet National Forest

The Chequamegon-Nicolet National Forest offers endless outdoor adventure possibilities. With over a million acres of forests, lakes, rivers, and wetlands, visitors can hike, camp, fish, and observe wildlife.

Adventure 105: Explore the Door County Coastal Byway

The Door County Coastal Byway is a scenic drive along the Door Peninsula. The route offers breathtaking views of Lake

Michigan, scenic landscapes, and diverse wildlife. There are plenty of stops along the way for hiking, birdwatching, and picnicking.

Adventure 106: Visit the Wildwood Wildlife Park and Nature Center in Minocqua

The Wildwood Wildlife Park and Nature Center (10094 WI-70, Minocqua, WI 54548) is home to over 750 animals, making it the largest zoo in Northwoods. It provides an engaging and educational wildlife experience for all ages, with opportunities to feed and interact with some animals.

Adventure 107: Explore the Lower Wisconsin Riverway

The Lower Wisconsin Riverway is a 92-mile stretch of the Wisconsin River, offering fantastic opportunities for canoeing, birdwatching, and wildlife viewing. Sandbars along the river provide perfect spots for picnics or overnight camping.

Adventure 108: Visit the Woodland Dunes Nature Center in Two Rivers

The Woodland Dunes Nature Center consists of over 1,500 acres of marshes, forests, and prairies. It's a haven for bird-watchers and nature enthusiasts, and the visitor center offers educational exhibits and programs.

Adventure 109: Hiking in the Tiffany Wildlife Area

The Tiffany Wildlife Area, covering over 13,000 acres, is one of the largest floodplain forests in the Midwest. It offers miles of hiking trails, excellent opportunities for birdwatching, and sightings of white-tailed deer and wild turkeys.

Adventure 110: Explore Governor Dodge State Park

Governor Dodge State Park (4175 WI-23, Dodgeville, WI 53533) offers diverse activities like hiking, fishing, boating, and camping. The park's ecosystems support a variety of wildlife, and the park's two lakes and numerous scenic spots make it a popular destination.

Adventure 111: Birdwatching at the Bay Beach Wildlife Sanctuary in Green Bay

The Bay Beach Wildlife Sanctuary (1660 East Shore Drive Green Bay, WI 54302) is a 600-acre urban wildlife refuge offering live animal exhibits, educational displays, miles of hiking trails, and excellent birdwatching opportunities. It's home to the state's largest wildlife rehabilitation program.

Adventure 112: Visit Schlitz Audubon Nature Center in Milwaukee

Schlitz Audubon Nature Center (1111 E Brown Deer Rd, Bayside, WI 53217), located on the shores of Lake

Michigan, offers six miles of trails through diverse habitats. Visitors can climb a 60-foot observation tower for stunning views, encounter a variety of resident raptor birds, and explore interactive exhibits in the nature center.

Chapter 10

Outdoor Adventures

The great state of Wisconsin is known for its picturesque landscapes and abundant outdoor activities. It's a place where natural beauty meets adventure, offering a myriad of exciting experiences from the calm waters of its lakes and rivers to the undulating hills of its countryside. In this chapter, we will take you through thrilling outdoor adventures in Wisconsin that cater to adrenaline junkies, tranquillity seekers, and everyone in between. We invite you to immerse yourself in the expansive outdoors and experience the thrill that Wisconsin's nature has to offer.

Adventure 113: Whitewater Rafting on the Menominee River

Experience the thrill of whitewater rafting on the Menominee River. With class IV rapids, this is an adrenaline-pumping adventure not to be missed. Numerous outfitters provide guided tours for beginners and experts alike, ensuring a fun and safe experience.

Adventure 114: Horseback Riding in the Southern Kettle Moraine State Forest

Explore the stunning Southern Kettle Moraine State Forest on horseback. The park has over 160 miles of trails that wind through a variety of terrains. Whether you're a novice rider or an experienced equestrian, there's a trail for you.

Adventure 115: Mountain Biking in Levis Mound Recreational Area

Levis Mound Recreational Area is a mountain biker's dream, with miles of trails that cater to all skill levels. From smooth single-track trails to challenging downhill sections, the area is known for its diverse and well-maintained trails.

Adventure 116: Rush River Ice Sculptures, Maiden Rock

In the tranquil town of Maiden Rock, a fascinating winter tradition unfolds. Every winter, the Rush River Ice Sculptures (N2696 Cty. Rd. A., Maiden Rock, WI 54750) transform the banks of the Rush River into an ethereal wonderland. This outdoor gallery showcases exquisite works of art made of ice sparkling under the winter sun. Ensure you're bundled up warm and bring a thermos of hot cocoa to enjoy this chilly, yet charming Wisconsin winter spectacle.

Adventure 117: ATV Riding in the Jackson County Forest

The Jackson County Forest is a fantastic location for ATV enthusiasts, offering more than 100 miles of scenic trails. The forest is open to ATV use year-round, and trails offer a mix of terrain types and difficulty levels.

Adventure 118: Skydiving in East Troy

For the ultimate adrenaline rush, experience the exhilaration of skydiving in East Troy. Professional instructors will guide you through every step, ensuring a thrilling and safe experience. The moment of free-fall followed by a peaceful parachute descent offers unparalleled views of Wisconsin's landscapes.

Adventure 119: Canyoneering in Pattison State Park

Canyoneering in Pattison State Park (6294 WI-35, Superior, WI 54880) offers an exciting outdoor adventure combining hiking, climbing, and swimming. Traverse the gorges carved by the Black River, enjoy the thrilling rappel down the cliffs, and take in the beauty of Wisconsin's tallest waterfall, Big Manitou Falls.

Adventure 120: Rock Climbing at Devil's Lake

Devil's Lake is a popular destination for rock climbers. With routes that cater to all skill levels, it's an excellent spot for beginners to learn the ropes and for experts to challenge themselves. The stunning views from the top are a rewarding bonus.

Adventure 121: Fly Fishing on the Bois Brule River

Bois Brule River, also known as the "River of Presidents," is a world-class destination for fly fishing. It is home to a variety of fish, including brook trout, brown trout, and steelhead, providing an ideal setting for both novices and experienced anglers.

Adventure 122: Snowshoeing in the Northern Highland-American Legion State Forest

Covering more than 225,000 acres, the Northern Highland-American Legion State Forest offers endless opportunities for snowshoeing. The park's extensive trail system winds through dense forests, across frozen lakes, and past scenic overlooks, offering a peaceful winter escape.

Give a man a fish, and you'll feed him for the whole day.
Teach a man to fish, and you'll get rid of him for the whole weekend!

Adventure 123: Kayaking on the Kickapoo River

The Kickapoo River, with its gentle flow and stunning rock formations, is an ideal location for a kayaking adventure. The river meanders through the heart of the Driftless Area, offering paddlers a chance to experience the region's unspoiled natural beauty.

Adventure 124: Caving in the Ledge View Nature Center

Explore the mysteries of the underground world in the Ledge View Nature Center's caves. Equipped with a helmet and a headlamp, visitors can crawl through passageways, discover fascinating rock formations, and learn about the cave's geology and history. The Ledge View Nature Center is located at: W2348 Short Rd, Chilton, WI 53014.

Adventure 125: Ice Fishing on Lake Winnebago

Lake Winnebago, Wisconsin's largest inland lake, is a popular destination for ice fishing. The lake is known for its walleye, perch, and sturgeon, and local outfitters can provide all the equipment and guidance you need for a successful fishing adventure.

Adventure 126: Snowmobiling in the Eagle River Area

Eagle River Area, known as the "Snowmobile Capital of the World," offers over 500 miles of well-groomed snowmobile trails. With picturesque winter landscapes and numerous cozy lodges along the way, it's a must-visit destination for snowmobiling enthusiasts.

Adventure 127: Paddle-boarding on Lake Monona

Stand-up paddle-boarding on Lake Monona offers a fun and relaxing way to enjoy Madison's beautiful skyline. Whether you're practicing yoga on a paddle-board or simply gliding across the water, it's a unique perspective of the city's beauty.

Adventure 128: Skiing at Mount La Crosse

Mount La Crosse (Old Town Hall Rd, La Crosse, WI 54601) is a haven for skiers, offering runs for all ability levels, from beginners to experts. With well-groomed slopes, a terrain park, and night skiing options, it's an ideal destination for a winter adventure.

Adventure 129: Kiteboarding on Lake Michigan

For an adrenaline-pumping water adventure, try kite-boarding on Lake Michigan. Harnessing the power of the wind, riders glide across the water on a board, pulling off jumps and tricks. Various outfitters offer lessons for beginners.

Adventure 130: Fat Tire Biking in the Chequamegon Area Mountain Bike Association (CAMBA) Trails

Experience the thrill of fat tire biking on the snow-covered trails of the Chequamegon Area Mountain Bike Association (CAMBA). The wide tires provide excellent traction on snow, making it a fun winter activity for cyclists.

Adventure 131: Cross-Country Skiing in Nine Mile Forest

Nine Mile Forest is renowned for its extensive network of cross-country skiing trails. Whether you prefer classic or skate skiing, the well-groomed trails provide a peaceful and invigorating winter experience amidst beautiful forested scenery.

Adventure 132: Sailing on Lake Geneva

Sailing on Lake Geneva offers a serene way to enjoy the lake's beauty. With numerous boat rental services, you can set sail and enjoy the tranquillity of the water, the warm summer breeze, and the picturesque shoreline.

Adventure 133: Zip-lining in Lake Geneva Canopy Tours

For a unique aerial adventure, experience the thrill of zip-lining at Lake Geneva Canopy Tours (N3232 Co Rd H, Lake Geneva, WI 53147). Glide through the treetops, cross suspended bridges, and enjoy breathtaking views of the surrounding forest.

Adventure 134: Camping in the Nicolet National Forest

Immerse yourself in nature by camping in the Nicolet National Forest. The forest offers numerous campsites, ranging from fully developed campgrounds to primitive backcountry sites. Enjoy hiking, fishing, and stargazing far away from the city's hustle and bustle.

Adventure 135: Create a Wisconsin Outdoor Adventure Passport

Create a Wisconsin Outdoor Adventure Passport, a free interactive guide that encourages the whole family to explore the state's diverse outdoor spaces. The passport can feature a collection of hiking trails, biking routes, waterfalls, and scenic viewpoints. Travelers can mark off their visits to each location, unlocking fun facts and interesting tidbits along the way. This passport serves as a motivator for individuals to discover Wisconsin's natural wonders, promote physical activity, and foster a deeper connection with the great outdoors, all while highlighting the state's commitment to conservation and sustainable tourism.

Chapter 11

Seasonal Adventures

In Wisconsin, each season paints a unique palette on the state's expansive landscapes and brings distinct opportunities for outdoor adventures. In this chapter, we explore seasonal adventures that capture the essence of Wisconsin's four seasons, taking you from the freshness of spring to the cozy winter days. While the beauty of Wisconsin transcends all seasons, there's something incredibly captivating about experiencing its outdoor wonders when they're at their peak. Let's embark on an exploration of these seasonally-special adventures, celebrating the natural rhythm and beauty of Wisconsin.

Adventure 136: Spring Wildflower Walks in Governor Nelson State Park

With the arrival of spring, Governor Nelson State Park (5140 Co Hwy M, Waunakee, WI 53597) transforms into a blooming paradise, teeming with vibrant wildflowers. Meandering through the park's trails presents an opportunity to witness the resurgence of life after the winter chill, from trilliums to wild geraniums, lending an ethereal beauty to your walks.

Adventure 137: Birdwatching at Honey Creek State Natural Area

Honey Creek State Natural Area (Skyview Rd, Loganville, WI 53943) is a paradise for bird enthusiasts. As migratory birds return in the spring, visitors can spot over a hundred different bird species, from vibrant warblers to majestic hawks. The chorus of birdsong echoing through the forest is a melody that resonates with the spirit of spring.

Adventure 138: Cherry Blossom Viewing in Sturgeon Bay

Spring in Sturgeon Bay ushers in a spectacular display of cherry blossoms. Rows of cherry trees adorned in delicate pink flowers create a breathtaking panorama against the backdrop of serene Lake Michigan. This beautiful spectacle is an ode to the rejuvenating energy of spring.

Adventure 139: Summer Hiking in the Coulee Experimental State Forest

As the temperature rises, Coulee Experimental State Forest offers stunning hiking trails, complete with panoramic views of the driftless area's rugged terrain. The lush greenery of summer amplifies the forest's beauty, making it a perfect location for a day of hiking and picnicking.

Adventure 140: Tubing Down the Sugar River

For a leisurely summer activity, rent a tube and float down the calm, meandering Sugar River. With the warm sun overhead and the gentle current guiding your path, it's a relaxing and fun way to cool down and enjoy Wisconsin's summer beauty.

Adventure 141: Berry Picking at a Local Farm

Wisconsin's summer season is the perfect time for berry picking. Local farms offer the opportunity to pick your strawberries, raspberries, and blackberries. This hands-on adventure provides not just a bucket full of fresh, juicy berries, but a deeper appreciation for the state's agricultural bounty.

Adventure 142: Canoeing on the Namekagon River

Summer is an ideal time to explore the clear, winding waters of the Namekagon River. Paddle at your own pace, soaking in the sights and sounds of the season, and cool off with a refreshing swim in one of the river's calm pools.

Adventure 143: Biking through the Blooming Prairie

With wildflowers blooming and the grasses growing tall, summer presents the perfect time to bike through Wisconsin's prairies. Trails such as the Capital City State Trail take you through a variety of landscapes, allowing you to enjoy the vibrant colors and warm breezes of a Wisconsin summer.

Adventure 144: Fall Foliage Hike in the Wyalusing State Park

When fall descends on Wisconsin, Wyalusing State Park (13081 State Park Ln, Bagley, WI 53801) dons a spectacular array of colors. Hiking through the park during this time is a visual treat, with the trails offering breathtaking views of the leaf-peeping spectacle that the forests of Wisconsin are famous for.

Adventure 145: Apple Picking in the Kickapoo Valley

Autumn in the Kickapoo Valley brings a harvest of crisp, juicy apples. Visit a local orchard for an apple picking adventure, a delightful activity for all ages. Enjoy the experience of picking your apples and savoring them fresh off the tree.

Where the Circus Began!

**Step right up!
The first circus in the United
States started in Delavan,
Wisconsin!**

Adventure 146: Pumpkin Festival in the Chippewa Valley

Celebrate fall in Wisconsin by attending a local pumpkin festival. Events like these, often held in the scenic Chippewa Valley, feature pumpkin carving contests, hayrides, corn mazes, and more. It's a fantastic way to immerse yourself in the festive spirit of the season.

Adventure 147: Cranberry Harvest in Warrens

Fall is cranberry harvest time in Wisconsin. In Warrens, you can watch as fields are flooded and the vibrant red berries float to the surface. Participate in a harvest tour to learn about the process, history, and impact of cranberry farming in Wisconsin.

Adventure 148: Stargazing at Newport State Park

Newport State Park (475 County Rd NP, Ellison Bay, WI 54210), a designated International Dark Sky Park, offers exceptional stargazing opportunities. With the cool, clear autumn nights, visitors can enjoy spectacular views of the Milky Way, distant galaxies, and an array of stars like never before.

Adventure 149: Ice Sculpture Festival in Rice Lake

Winter in Wisconsin is the season of ice and snow, and what better way to celebrate it than by visiting an ice sculpture festival? In Rice Lake, artists transform blocks of ice into incredible works of art, creating a magical winter wonderland that's a feast for the eyes.

Adventure 150: Winter Wildlife Tracking in Perrot State Park

Perrot State Park (26247 Sullivan Rd, Trempealeau, WI 54661), with its dense forests and steep bluffs, is an excellent place for winter wildlife tracking. The fresh snow reveals the tracks of deer, foxes, and many bird species, offering a silent yet compelling narrative of the creatures that thrive in Wisconsin's winter.

Adventure 151: Snow Sculpting in the City of Delafield

Join in the winter fun at the annual snow sculpting event in Delafield. Participants carve enormous blocks of snow into stunning sculptures. Whether you're an observer or a participant, the event is a celebration of Wisconsin's winter creativity.

Adventure 152: Ice Skating on Mirror Lake

Mirror Lake transforms into a winter wonderland once frozen over, providing a beautiful and spacious area for ice skating. Lace up your skates and glide across the glassy surface, surrounded by the snowy beauty of the lake's natural scenery.

Adventure 153: Winter Hiking in the Blue Hills

Experience the quiet beauty of winter by hiking in the Blue Hills. With a fresh coat of snow covering the landscape, the hills offer a serene setting for a winter hike. Witness the majestic icicle formations and enjoy the tranquility of a winter's day in the forest.

Adventure 154: Christmas in Cedarburg

Nothing captures the enchantment of the holiday season quite like the town of Cedarburg, Wisconsin. Cedarburg transforms into a scene straight out of a Hallmark movie, offering a quintessential Midwestern Christmas experience that can warm even the coldest winter day. The town's historic downtown, already charming, becomes a wonderland adorned with thousands of twinkling lights, festooned wreaths, and cheerfully decorated storefronts. A visit to Cedarburg during the Christmas season is an unforgettable journey into the heart of holiday spirit.

Adventure 155: Snowshoeing in the Mukwonago River Unit

The Mukwonago River Unit, a part of the Southern Kettle Moraine State Forest, is a great location for snowshoeing. Trek through snow-covered meadows and hardwood forests, and experience the peaceful beauty of Wisconsin's winter landscapes.

Adventure 156: Experience Thrills and Chills on the Dells Ghost Boat

As the chill of autumn envelops Wisconsin, experience a thrilling, seasonal adventure aboard the Dells Ghost Boat (11 Broadway Ave, Wisconsin Dells, WI 53965). This eerie journey on the Wisconsin River invites brave souls to discover the mysterious legends and haunted tales of the river's hidden canyons. The chilling stories, combined with the spooky ambience of the boat ride, make this adventure an unforgettable part of Wisconsin's fall festivities.

Adventure 157: Winter Camping in Black River State Forest

For the true adventure enthusiast, winter camping in the Black River State Forest can be an unforgettable experience. While it may be a challenging adventure, the reward of experiencing the quiet solitude of the forest blanketed in snow is well worth it.

Adventure 158: Eagle Watching on the Mississippi River

Winter is the prime time for bald eagle watching along the Mississippi River. The open water provides a perfect fishing ground for eagles, offering visitors the opportunity to observe these majestic birds in their natural habitat.

Chapter 12

Sports Adventures

Wisconsin's diverse landscape and enthusiastic communities lend themselves to a broad range of sports adventures. From water sports on its many lakes and rivers to rock climbing on its rugged bluffs, Wisconsin presents ample opportunities for sporting excitement. Whether you're an avid athlete or a casual participant, the state has something to suit every skill level and interest. This chapter will take you on a journey through sports adventures that celebrate Wisconsin's athletic spirit.

Adventure 159: Sailing on Lake Koshkonong

Lake Koshkonong, one of the largest inland lakes in Wisconsin, offers excellent conditions for sailing. Enjoy a day on the water, navigating through the lake's diverse sections that range from wide open spaces to smaller channels lined with lush vegetation.

Adventure 160: Rock Climbing at Devil's Punchbowl

Devil's Punchbowl Preserve (410th St, Menomonie, WI 54751) offers challenging rock climbing opportunities. The high sandstone cliffs require skill and determination, rewarding climbers with stunning views of the surrounding landscapes and the bowl-shaped depression that gives the location its name.

Adventure 161: White-Water Rafting on the Peshtigo River

The Peshtigo River offers some of the best white-water rafting experiences in the Midwest. With a variety of rapids ranging from class II to IV, this river caters to both novice and experienced rafters, promising an adrenaline-filled adventure on its surging waters.

Adventure 162: Disc Golf at Standing Rocks Park

Standing Rocks Park in Portage County (7695 Standing Rocks Rd, Stevens Point, WI 54481) boasts one of the finest disc golf courses in the state. This 18-hole course winds through a varied landscape, challenging players with its intricate design and the need for strategic play. The game combines a walk in the park with the competitive thrill of sports.

Adventure 163: Snowboarding at Tyrol Basin

Located in Dane County, Tyrol Basin is a popular destination for winter sports. Snowboarders can enjoy the well-maintained slopes, which offer a variety of runs to suit different skill levels, from gentle hills for beginners to more challenging terrains for advanced riders.

Adventure 164: Skydiving in Sturtevant

Experience the thrill of skydiving with a jump over the scenic Sturtevant area. As you free-fall, you'll enjoy a bird's eye view of the beautiful landscapes below, making for an unforgettable adventure. This activity is guided by professionals to ensure your safety while providing the thrill of a lifetime.

Adventure 165: Surfing in Sheboygan

Known as the 'Malibu of the Midwest', Sheboygan offers ideal conditions for surfing. The city's location on the western shore of Lake Michigan results in consistent waves, attracting surfers of all skill levels. This unlikely surfing hotspot promises a unique Wisconsin sports adventure.

Adventure 166: Golfing at Erin Hills

Erin Hills Golf Course (7169 Co Rd O, Hartford, WI 53027), home to the 2017 U.S. Open, is a must-visit destination for golf enthusiasts. The sprawling course, with its rolling terrain and challenging holes, offers an enjoyable and strategic golfing experience, all while providing panoramic views of the beautiful Wisconsin countryside.

Adventure 167: Soccer Match at Breese Stevens Field

Breese Stevens Field (917 E Mifflin St, Madison, WI 53703) hosts exciting soccer matches throughout the season. Join the local crowd to cheer on the home team, Forward Madison FC, and immerse yourself in the electrifying atmosphere of a live soccer game.

Adventure 168: Inline Skating on Glacial Drumlin State Trail

Glacial Drumlin State Trail, stretching from Waukesha to Cottage Grove, offers a smooth, paved surface perfect for inline skating. This 52-mile trail winds through scenic farmland, woods, and wetlands, making for a picturesque skating experience.

Don't Hold Your Breath!

The waitlist for Green Bay Packers season tickets includes around 147,000 names, with an estimated wait time of 30 years.

Adventure 169: Archery at Root River Archery Range

The Root River Archery Range (4820 6 Mile Rd, Racine, WI 53402) in Racine County offers a challenging course for archery enthusiasts. The range features targets at varying distances and elevations, simulating hunting scenarios and offering archers a unique, skill-building experience.

Adventure 170: Kiteboarding on Lake Mendota

Lake Mendota's wide-open water and favorable wind conditions make it an ideal location for kiteboarding. Whether you're an experienced rider or a first-timer, the thrill of harnessing the wind's power to glide across the lake's surface is an adventure you won't forget.

Adventure 171: Curling in the Milwaukee Curling Club

Embrace Wisconsin's winter spirit by trying your hand at curling in the Milwaukee Curling Club (W67N890 Washington Ave, Cedarburg, WI 53012), the oldest curling club in continuous existence in the United States. Here, you can learn the intricacies of this ice sport, which combines strategy and skill in a unique blend of athleticism and camaraderie.

Adventure 172: Kayaking on the Rock River

Paddle your way along the scenic Rock River that winds through Southern Wisconsin. The river's calm waters and abundant wildlife make it an ideal destination for kayaking, offering a tranquil adventure amidst nature.

Adventure 173: Trap Shooting at Waukesha Gun Club

Try your hand at trap shooting at the Waukesha Gun Club (N22W23170 Watertown Rd, Waukesha, WI 53188). This sport involves shooting at clay targets launched from a house located in front of the shooter. It's an excellent opportunity to test your accuracy and reflexes while enjoying a day out in the field.

Adventure 174: Volleyball at Bradford Beach

Bradford Beach in Milwaukee is a popular spot for beach volleyball. With numerous courts set up in the summer, it's a fantastic place to join a pickup game or organize a match with friends. The sand, sun, and the lake's beautiful backdrop add to the overall experience, making it a vibrant and fun-filled adventure.

Adventure 175: Mountain Biking in Quarry Park

Quarry Park (3102 Stevens St, Madison, WI 53705) offers mountain biking enthusiasts a thrilling adventure. The park's terrain includes rocky paths and challenging climbs, making it perfect for riders looking to test their skills. Navigating these trails offers a heart-pounding ride amid a beautiful forest setting.

Adventure 176: Waterskiing on Pewaukee Lake

Pewaukee Lake, located in Waukesha County, is a favorite spot for waterskiing. The large, clean lake offers calm conditions, making it perfect for both beginners learning the ropes and experienced skiers practicing their tricks. Enjoy a day of waterskiing under the warm summer sun for a classic Wisconsin sports adventure.

Adventure 177: Basketball Game at the Fiserv Forum

Basketball fans can catch a live NBA game at the Fiserv Forum (1111 Vel R. Phillips Ave, Milwaukee, WI 53203), home of the Milwaukee Bucks. The energy and excitement of watching a professional basketball match live, surrounded by thousands of passionate fans, is an experience unlike any other.

Adventure 178: Canoeing on the Fox River

The Fox River, with its gentle flow and abundant natural beauty, provides excellent conditions for a canoeing adventure. Paddling on this river offers a peaceful journey, allowing you to take in the wildlife, the riparian landscapes, and the occasional small town along the way.

Adventure 179: National Bobblehead Hall of Fame and Museum

For sports enthusiasts and collectors alike, the National Bobblehead Hall of Fame and Museum (170 S 1st St 2nd floor, Milwaukee, WI 53204) promises an adventure like no other. This quirky museum houses the world's largest collection of bobbleheads, boasting more than 6,500 figures on display. As you step inside, you'll be greeted by a colorful array of bobbleheads from every genre you can imagine - not just sports! Icons of pop culture, politics, entertainment, and even special commemorative editions all have a home here.

Adventure 180: Ice Hockey at the Alliant Energy Center

The Alliant Energy Center (1919 Alliant Energy Center Way, Madison, WI 53713) regularly hosts ice hockey games. Whether you're cheering on a local team or participating in a friendly match, playing or watching this fast-paced, exciting sport is an adventure not to be missed.

Adventure 181: Wind Surfing on Lake Superior

Lake Superior, with its large expanse and strong winds, provides excellent conditions for windsurfing. Enjoy the thrill of gliding across the water propelled by the wind, with the awe-inspiring vistas of the lake surrounding you.

Chapter 13

Spotlight: The Washington Island Stavkirke

If you take a short ferry ride from the mainland to Washington Island, Wisconsin, you'll come across a sight that seems straight out of a history book – a medieval Norwegian church! This unique structure, known as a stavkirke, was hand-built by the local Lutheran Church in 1991 and has been carefully maintained ever since. But here's the kicker: a visit today will transport you back in time to the days of the Vikings!

Stavkirke churches were once a common sight across Europe during the Middle Ages, especially around the year 1150 AD. The name comes from the Old Norse word "stafr," which refers to the load-bearing ore-pine posts that make up the church's structure. The design of the Washington Island Stavkirke is a fascinating blend of Christian and Viking styles, making it a true one-of-a-kind experience.

At the height of their popularity, there were about 1,300 stavkirke churches scattered throughout Europe. However, most of them have been lost to fire or rot over the centuries due to their wooden construction. This makes the Washington Island Stavkirke an even more special find – it's a rare chance to see a piece of medieval history right here in Wisconsin!

As you explore the grounds of the stavkirke, you'll find yourself surrounded by a sense of peace and tranquility. Benches and Bible verses dot the landscape, inviting you to take a moment to reflect and appreciate the beauty of this unique place. The inside of the church is just as intriguing as the outside, with authentic construction that transports you back in time.

Whether you're a history buff, an architecture enthusiast, or simply someone who loves discovering new and exciting places, the Washington Island Stavkirke is sure to delight you. This little slice of medieval Norway in the middle of Wisconsin is a true wonder that everyone should experience at least once. So why not plan a visit and see for yourself what makes this church so special? You won't be disappointed!

The Washington Island Stavkirke stands as a testament to the power of preservation and the importance of keeping history alive. Thanks to the dedication of the local Lutheran Church and the community, this incredible structure will continue to inspire and amaze visitors for generations to come. It's a shining example of how we can all work together to protect and celebrate the wonders of our world, one piece of history at a time. Happy travels!

Chapter 14

Culinary Adventures

Wisconsin is a state of culinary abundance and diversity, a place where food lovers can embark on a gastronomic adventure that combines tradition with innovation, local with global, and comfort with novelty. Its bounty ranges from fresh produce grown on local farms, award-winning cheeses, and a rich heritage of beer brewing to international cuisine influenced by a mix of cultures. This chapter takes you on a journey of culinary adventures across the state, each adventure a feast for your senses and a celebration of Wisconsin's food culture.

Adventure 182: Brunch at Mint Mark in Madison

Begin your culinary exploration at Mint Mark (1929 Winnebago St, Madison, WI 53704), a quaint eatery located in Madison. Famous for its inventive brunch menu, Mint Mark blends local ingredients to create dishes with vibrant flavors. From savory egg-based dishes to sweet delights such as ricotta pancakes, your taste buds are bound to embark on a journey of their own.

Adventure 183: Wine Tasting at Wollersheim Winery & Distillery

Situated on a scenic hillside overlooking the Wisconsin River, Wollersheim Winery & Distillery (7876 WI-188, Prairie Du Sac, WI 53578) offers an exquisite wine tasting experience. The winery's award-winning wines range from bold reds to crisp whites and delightful rosés. Paired with an educational tour of the winery, this adventure combines knowledge, taste, and scenery.

Adventure 184: Cheese Tasting at Fromagination in Madison

No culinary adventure in Wisconsin would be complete without a cheese tasting. Visit Fromagination (12 S Carroll St, Madison, WI 53703), a specialty cheese shop located in Madison. Here, you can taste artisanal cheeses from across the state, each unique in flavor, texture, and aroma. Pair your selection with gourmet crackers and preserves for a heavenly cheese experience.

Adventure 185: Wood-Fired Pizza at Wild Tomato in Fish Creek

Visit Wild Tomato Wood-Fired Pizza and Grille (4023 WI-42, Fish Creek, WI 54212) for some of the best wood-fired pizza in Wisconsin. Using fresh, locally sourced ingredients, these handcrafted pizzas are a treat for all pizza lovers. The crispy crust, tangy tomato sauce, and flavorful toppings come together in a symphony of taste.

Adventure 186: Cherry Pie at Seaquist Orchards in Sister Bay

Indulge in a slice of cherry pie at Seaquist Orchards Farm Market (11482 WI-42, Sister Bay, WI 54234). Known for their homegrown cherries, Seaquist Orchards' pies are baked fresh daily. The perfectly balanced sweet-tart filling nestled in a flaky, buttery crust makes this pie a not-to-miss culinary delight.

Adventure 187: Craft Beer Tasting at Ale Asylum in Madison

Visit Ale Asylum (3698 Kinsman Blvd, Madison, WI 53704) for an immersive craft beer experience. With a rotating selection of artisanal brews on tap, Ale Asylum offers a beer style for every palate. From hop-heavy IPAs to smooth, rich stouts, the tasting journey here is an adventure in flavor and craft.

Adventure 188: The Cheeze Factory is a Vegan's Paradise

Embrace your love for cheese at the Cheeze Factory Restaurant (618 Oak St, Baraboo, WI 53913). This unique dining establishment proudly celebrates Wisconsin's cheese culture with a twist: everything on the menu is vegan! From dairy-free, plant-based creations to an array of delightful vegan desserts, the Cheeze Factory caters to every palate, including those adhering to a vegan lifestyle. Their innovative take on traditional cuisine makes it a must-visit destination for food lovers seeking a taste adventure in Wisconsin's culinary scene.

Adventure 189: Fresh Seafood at Harbor House in Milwaukee

For an elegant seafood dining experience, visit Harbor House (550 N Harbor Dr, Milwaukee, WI 53202). Overlooking Lake Michigan, the restaurant offers an extensive menu of fresh seafood, from delicate scallops to flavorful lobster. Complement your meal with a glass of wine and take in the breathtaking waterfront views.

Adventure 190: Cider Tasting at Maiden Rock Apples Winery & Cidery

Located in the beautiful Mississippi River Valley, Maiden Rock Apples Winery & Cidery (W12266 King Ln, Stockholm, WI 54769) offers a variety of handcrafted ciders for tasting. These crisp, refreshing ciders, made from locally grown apples, are a testament to the region's rich apple-growing heritage.

Adventure 191: Bratwurst at Usinger's Famous Sausage in Milwaukee

Usinger's Famous Sausage (1030 N Dr. Martin Luther King Jr. Drive, Milwaukee, WI 53203) is a mecca for sausage lovers. Here, you can enjoy the state's iconic bratwurst, made from time-tested, family recipes. Savor the juicy, flavorful bratwurst served in a hearty bun, a staple of Wisconsin's culinary identity.

A Bratwurst Haven!

Sheboygan, Wisconsin isn't just a city: it's the "Bratwurst Capital of the World!" Brat lovers, rejoice!

Adventure 192: Chocolate Tour at Kohler Chocolates

Indulge your sweet tooth with a tour of Kohler Chocolates (725 Woodlake Rd # D, Kohler, WI 53044), a premier chocolatier in the state. Discover the art of chocolate making, from the selection of fine ingredients to the crafting of beautiful, delectable chocolates. The highlight, of course, is the tasting – a chance to savor the rich, luxurious flavor of these handcrafted confections.

Adventure 193: Cooking Class at Orange Tree Imports in Madison

For hands-on culinary enthusiasts, take a cooking class at Orange Tree Imports (1721 Monroe St, Madison, WI 53711). Whether you're a novice or an experienced cook, these classes offer a chance to learn new techniques, recipes, and cuisines under the guidance of professional chefs. It's an adventure that culminates in the satisfaction of a meal prepared by your own hands.

Adventure 194: Ice Cream at Kopp's Frozen Custard

Enjoy a sweet, creamy treat at Kopp's Frozen Custard (18880 W Bluemound Rd, Brookfield, WI 53045), a beloved ice cream shop that has been serving Wisconsin since the 1950s. Their rotating selection of flavors, made fresh daily, ensures there's always something new to try. From classics like vanilla and chocolate to unique combinations like banana cream pie and blueberry muffin, there's a flavor for everyone.

Adventure 195: Friday Fish Fry at Lakefront Brewery

Lakefront Brewery (1872 N Commerce St, Milwaukee, WI 53212) offers a quintessential Wisconsin experience with its Friday Fish Fry. The beer-battered fish, served with coleslaw and rye bread, is a local tradition. Complement your meal with one of the brewery's craft beers for a truly Wisconsinite experience.

Adventure 196: Cranberry Marsh Tour and Tasting at Wisconsin Cranberry Discovery Center

Discover the tart-sweet joy of Wisconsin's state fruit on a cranberry marsh tour at the Wisconsin Cranberry Discovery Center and Cranberry Country Cafe (204 Main Street,

Warrens, WI 54666). Learn about the history of cranberry farming in the state, watch the cranberries being harvested, and of course, sample fresh cranberries and cranberry products, from juices to sauces.

Adventure 197: Dining at Ardent in Milwaukee

Treat yourself to an elevated dining experience at Ardent (1751 N Farwell Ave, Milwaukee, WI 53202), a restaurant known for its innovative approach to Midwestern cuisine. The intimate, relaxed setting belies the complexity and sophistication of the dishes, which showcase locally-sourced ingredients in surprising and delightful ways.

Adventure 198: Apple Picking and Cider Tasting at Brightonwoods Orchard

For a true taste of fall, head to Brightonwoods Orchard (1072 288th Ave, Burlington, WI 53105). Pick your own apples from the dozens of varieties grown on the farm, and then head to the cidery for a tasting. The orchard's own apple cider, both sweet and hard versions, is a must-try.

Adventure 199: Beer Cheese Soup at The Old Fashioned in Madison

For a comforting, Wisconsin-style meal, enjoy a bowl of beer cheese soup at The Old Fashioned (23 N Pinckney St #1, Madison, WI 53703). This popular dish combines two Wisconsin staples, beer and cheese, into a hearty, flavorful soup. Served with a side of crusty bread, it's the perfect dish to warm up a cold day.

Adventure 200: Authentic German Cuisine at Mader's Restaurant in Milwaukee

Enjoy traditional German cuisine at Mader's Restaurant (1041 N Dr. Martin Luther King Jr. Dr, Milwaukee, WI 53203), one of Milwaukee's oldest and most beloved restaurants. From Wiener schnitzel to sauerbraten, each dish is prepared with care and served in a warm, inviting atmosphere, offering an authentic taste of Germany in the heart of Wisconsin.

Adventure 201: Gourmet Popcorn at Pop's Kettle Corn

Discover a fun and flavorsome treat at Pop's Kettle Corn (S75W17461 Janesville Rd, Muskego, WI 53150). With an array of unique flavors like buffalo ranch and caramel apple, this isn't your ordinary popcorn. Whether you prefer sweet or savory, this local popcorn shop is sure to have something that tickles your taste buds.

Adventure 202: Savor a Juicy Lucy at Monk's Bar & Grill

Experience the legendary Juicy Lucy at Monk's Bar & Grill (220 Broadway Ave, Wisconsin Dells, WI 53965). This unique twist on the classic cheeseburger has the cheese inside the meat, resulting in a gooey, melty center that elevates the humble burger to new heights of deliciousness.

Adventure 203: Baked goods at Rocket Baby Bakery in Milwaukee

Visit Rocket Baby Bakery (6822 W North Ave, Wauwatosa, WI 53213), a delightful artisan bakery in Milwaukee. Known for their European-style bread and pastries, every item is made from scratch with high-quality ingredients. Whether you're in the mood for a crusty baguette, a flaky croissant, or a sweet treat like a macaron or eclair, you're in for a treat.

Adventure 204: Dining at the Driftless Café

Nestled in the Driftless Area of southwestern Wisconsin, Driftless Café (118 W Court St, Viroqua, WI 54665) serves dishes made from the best local, organic, and sustainable ingredients. The ever-changing menu is a testament to the seasonality and diversity of Wisconsin's agricultural bounty, offering diners a truly local culinary experience.

Chapter 15

Shopping Adventures

As the great state of Wisconsin offers a wealth of fascinating attractions, it is also an enticing destination for those with a penchant for retail exploration. Whether you are searching for unique gifts, antiques, fresh local produce, or exceptional handicrafts, Wisconsin's diverse shopping landscape presents an array of choices. Each shopping adventure is not just an opportunity to buy but to explore, discover, and connect with the local community. The following selection of shopping adventures from all corners of Wisconsin will guide you to a diverse array of retail experiences from charming boutiques to bustling farmers markets.

Adventure 205: Browse the Antiques at Columbus Antique Mall & Museum

Known as "Wisconsin's Largest Antique Mall", the Columbus Antique Mall & Museum (239 Whitney St, Columbus, WI 53925) offers shoppers the chance to explore and purchase from an extensive collection of antiques and collectibles. With more than 200 dealers, the selection is vast, spanning a range of periods and styles. Every visit is like a treasure hunt, with the possibility of unearthing a unique piece of history.

Adventure 206: Explore the Boutiques of Historic Downtown Hudson

Stroll through the picturesque streets of Hudson's historic downtown area where you'll discover a plethora of unique boutiques. Find everything from trendy fashion and accessories to home decor, gourmet foods, and local art. The friendly shop owners are always ready to provide a warm welcome and help you find that perfect item.

Adventure 207: Foodie Fun at Dane County Farmers' Market

Although Madison's Farmers Market was previously mentioned, Dane County's other towns have their own bustling markets as well. In addition to a selection of fresh local produce, you'll find a diverse array of Wisconsin-made cheeses, artisan breads, jams, honey, and many other gourmet delights that reflect the region's culinary richness.

Adventure 208: Discover Handmade Goods at Morning Glory Gallery

Located within the Marcus Performing Arts Center (929 N Water St, Milwaukee, WI 53202), Morning Glory Gallery is a vibrant showcase for Wisconsin's fine craftspeople. The gallery features a wide array of items such as glass art, ceramics, jewelry, fiber art, and woodwork, all handcrafted by local artists. Whether you're looking for a special gift or a piece to add to your own collection, you'll find it here.

Adventure 209: Typewriter Hunting in Milwaukee

Milwaukee holds an iconic place in the annals of American history - it's the birthplace of the typewriter. For those with a love for antiques, nostalgia, or simply a passion for words, why not commemorate this iconic piece of Wisconsin history by hunting for a vintage typewriter of your own? Explore the city's myriad of second-hand stores and vintage shops for a chance to come across these storied machines. Imagine the thrill of stumbling upon an original Remington, the very first typewriter model produced by Milwaukee's E. Remington and Sons in 1873.

Adventure 210: High-End Shopping at Mayfair Mall

Mayfair Mall (2500 N Mayfair Rd, Wauwatosa, WI 53226) is the place to be for high-end shopping in Wisconsin. With a diverse selection of major retailers and designer boutiques, you're bound to find something to suit your style. From luxury fashion to state-of-the-art electronics, the choice is immense and the shopping experience is top-notch.

Adventure 211: Book Hunting at Boswell Book Company

A must-visit for book lovers, Boswell Book Company (2559 N Downer Ave, Milwaukee, WI 53211) is an independent bookstore with a charming, old-world vibe. The store offers a broad selection of books in all genres, and the staff is well known for their knowledgeable recommendations. You can also enjoy author readings and book club events for an immersive literary experience.

Adventure 212: Shop Local at La Pointe Farmers Market

Discover the fresh flavors of Madeline Island at the La Pointe Farmers Market (804 Fort Rd, La Pointe, WI 54850). This small market is big on local charm, offering a range of organic produce, artisanal cheeses, homemade jams, and handcrafted goods, all sourced from the island and surrounding area. Shopping here is not only a feast for the senses but also a great way to support local growers and producers.

Adventure 213: Explore Vintage Finds at Retro Revolution

Retro Revolution (3225 E Washington Ave B, Madison, WI 53704) is a treasure trove of vintage and retro items. From mid-century furniture to vintage clothing and accessories, vinyl records, and kitschy decor, this is the perfect place to find something truly unique and full of character.

Adventure 214: Crystal Shopping at Mimosa Books & Gifts

Mimosa Books & Gifts (409 State St, Madison, WI 53703) is a unique shop specializing in healing crystals, spiritual books, and metaphysical supplies. Whether you're an experienced crystal user or just curious, the friendly staff will help guide you to the perfect stones for your needs.

Adventure 215: Uncover Unique Gifts at Fischberger's Variety

Fischberger's Variety (2445 N Holton St, Milwaukee, WI 53212) is a fun, eclectic shop that specializes in quirky, hard-to-find items. Here you'll find everything from vintage toys and games to local artisan goods, funky home decor, and humorous gifts. It's the perfect place to find a unique souvenir or gift.

Adventure 216: Eclectic Fun at American Science and Surplus

For a shopping experience that's equal parts educational and entertaining, the American Science and Surplus store (6901 W Oklahoma Ave, Milwaukee, WI 53219) is an absolute must-visit. From science kits, military surplus, and educational toys to eclectic novelties, quirky home goods, and even genuine laboratory supplies, there's truly something for everyone. Shoppers often describe it as akin to stepping into a mad scientist's garage sale, where the unexpected becomes the norm.

Adventure 217: Indulge in Gourmet Chocolates at Wilmar Chocolates

For the chocolate lover, a visit to Wilmar Chocolates (1222 N Superior St, Appleton, WI 54911) is a must. This local chocolate shop has been crafting gourmet chocolates using old-world methods since 1956. Choose from a variety of delicious treats, or create your own custom chocolate bar with your choice of ingredients.

Adventure 218: Explore Unique Designs at Anthology

Anthology (230 State St, Madison, WI 53703) is a shop that specializes in handmade goods, many of which have a local or regional focus. Here, you'll find a vast array of unique items including paper goods, jewelry, home decor, and Wisconsin-themed merchandise. The store is also a hub for crafting workshops, offering the chance to learn new skills and make your own creations.

Adventure 219: Vintage Shopping at Second Chance Antiques and Collectibles

Venture into the past at Second Chance Antiques and Collectibles (7532 W Becher St, West Allis, WI 53219). This antique shop is filled with vintage furniture, jewelry, glassware, and collectibles. Whether you're a seasoned collector or just love the charm of older items, this shop is a treasure trove waiting to be explored.

Adventure 220: Shop for Gifts at Waxwing

Located in Milwaukee, Waxwing is a locally-focused shop featuring goods from over 300 artists, most of whom are from Wisconsin. From artwork and jewelry to candles and clothing, there are plenty of unique, handmade items to discover, making it a great place to find the perfect gift or a special treat for yourself.

Adventure 221: Unique Finds at Swoon

Swoon (5422 W Vliet St, Milwaukee, WI 53208) is a treasure trove of eclectic and unique items. This charming shop carries a range of merchandise including clothing, accessories, home decor, and vintage finds. Each item in the store has been carefully curated, offering a distinctive shopping experience.

Adventure 222: Handmade Jewelry at Canela-Canela

Canela-Canela (10412 N Baehr Rd, Mequon, WI 53092) is a jewelry boutique that offers beautifully handcrafted pieces. Each piece of jewelry is made on-site, offering a unique and personal touch. With a variety of styles and materials, there's something for everyone, whether you're looking for a new statement piece or a subtle accessory.

Adventure 223: Visit Mars Cheese Castle

In Kenosha, the Mars Cheese Castle is not just a store, it's a kingdom of cheese. The castle-like structure houses an immense variety of cheese, from classic Wisconsin cheddar to rare imported varieties. Besides cheese, they offer a selection of gourmet foods, bakery items, and Wisconsin-themed souvenirs. Mars Cheese Castle is located at: 2800 W Frontage Rd, Kenosha, WI 53144.

Adventure 224: Unique Goods at The Local Store

Located in downtown Eau Claire, The Local Store (205 N Dewey St, Eau Claire, WI 54703) is a community-focused shop featuring over 3000 items from local makers, artists, and authors. From handmade jewelry to artisan foods, Wisconsin-themed apparel, and home decor, you'll find a unique and thoughtful selection that celebrates the spirit of the region.

Adventure 225: Fair Trade Shopping at Global Gifts

Global Gifts (125 E State St, Burlington, WI 53105) offers a unique shopping experience focused on fair trade. Featuring handicrafts from artisans around the world, each item in the store tells a story of empowerment and sustainability. From jewelry to home decor and gifts, you can feel good knowing your purchases make a difference.

Adventure 226: Drift to the Drift Mercantile

Drift Mercantile (211 Pearl St, La Crosse, WI 54601) is a testament to Wisconsin's commitment to supporting local artisans and craftspeople. This unique shopping destination offers a variety of locally made products, from handcrafted jewelry to sustainable clothing and accessories, all reflecting the spirit and craftsmanship of the region. Picking up an item or two from Drift Mercantile is not only a way to remember your Wisconsin adventure but also a meaningful way to support the local economy and its creative residents.

Adventure 227: Farm Fresh at Viroqua Food Co-op

In the small town of Viroqua, the Viroqua Food Co-op (609 N Main St, Viroqua, WI 54665) is a destination for lovers of fresh, local food. Offering a large selection of organic and locally produced goods, you'll find everything from fresh produce to artisanal cheeses, fresh-baked bread, and locally raised meats. It's a food lover's paradise that also supports local farmers.

Chapter 16

Historical and Archaeological Adventures

Wisconsin is a state steeped in history and offers a multitude of historical and archaeological adventures that speak of its ancient Indigenous roots, rich maritime legacy, fascinating mining history, and time as a bustling hub of the fur trade. From well-preserved archaeological sites to grand historical buildings and museums, you can dive into the past and discover the events that have shaped the Wisconsin of today.

Adventure 228: Unearth the Mound Builders at Aztalan State Park

Aztalan State Park (N6200 County Rd Q, Jefferson, WI 53549), in Jefferson County, is home to one of the most important archaeological sites in Wisconsin. Once a fortified town, Aztalan offers a glimpse into the lifestyle of the Mississippians who settled here around AD 1000. Walk along the marked trails, observe the reconstructed stockade and platform mounds, and imagine life as it was in this bustling ancient community.

Adventure 229: Step Back in Time at Pendarvis Historic Site

Nestled in Mineral Point, the Pendarvis Historic Site (114 Shakerag St, Mineral Point, WI 53565) showcases the Cornish culture and mining history of Wisconsin. Here, you can wander through beautifully restored stone and log buildings that date back to the 1840s, when Cornish immigrants were drawn to the area's lead and zinc mining opportunities.

Adventure 230: Explore History at the Milwaukee Soldiers Home

The Milwaukee Soldiers Home (515 General Mitchell Blvd, Milwaukee, WI 53214), part of the Clement J. Zablocki VA Medical Center grounds, is a National Historic Landmark. Established after the Civil War to care for wounded veterans, the site boasts beautiful, restored Victorian Gothic buildings. A guided tour is an emotional journey that pays tribute to the sacrifices of American veterans.

Adventure 231: Visit the Astor Fur Warehouse

In the historic town of Prairie du Chien, the Astor Fur Warehouse (300-498 N Water St, Prairie du Chien, WI 53821) stands as a reminder of the bustling fur trade era. Constructed in 1828 by the American Fur Company, it was once a hub of activity. Today, this restored stone building displays exhibits about the fur trade and the significant role it played in the state's development.

Adventure 232: Roam the Streets of Historic Mineral Point

Mineral Point is one of the oldest cities in Wisconsin, filled with pre-Civil War architecture and historical charm. Wander down High Street, with its limestone buildings that house artisan studios, antique stores, and specialty shops, or join a historical walking tour to hear fascinating stories about the city's past.

Adventure 233: Dive into Maritime History at the Door County Maritime Museum

Located in Sturgeon Bay, the Door County Maritime Museum (120 N Madison Ave, Sturgeon Bay, WI 54235) traces Wisconsin's rich maritime heritage. The museum features exhibits on shipbuilding, lighthouses, and life-saving stations, and a highlight is the chance to tour the retired ship 'John Purves,' providing an up-close look at maritime life.

Adventure 234: Discover Wisconsin's Logging History

The Wisconsin Logging Museum (1110 E Half Moon Dr, Eau Claire, WI 54703) offers a fascinating glimpse into the life and work of Wisconsin's lumberjacks in the 1800s. Explore authentic recreated buildings, see vintage logging equipment, and learn about the state's logging history through interactive exhibits.

Adventure 235: Visit the H.H. Bennett Studio & History Center

In Wisconsin Dells, the H.H. Bennett Studio & History Center (215 Broadway Ave, Wisconsin Dells, WI 53965) introduces visitors to the man known as "the man who made Wisconsin Dells famous." Explore the 1875 photography studio where Bennett created stunning images of the Dells, using his inventive techniques, and helped to turn the region into a major tourist destination.

Adventure 236: Immerse in Pioneer Life at Stonefield Historic Site

Located in Cassville, the Stonefield Historic Site (12195 Co Hwy VV, Cassville, WI 53806) takes you back to the 1900s farming life in Wisconsin. Wander through the recreated farming village and admire the vintage agricultural machinery. Don't miss the Governor Nelson Dewey Home, the restored estate of Wisconsin's first governor.

Adventure 237: Stroll Through History in the Fifth Ward

Milwaukee's Fifth Ward, known as Walker's Point, is one of the city's oldest neighborhoods. A mix of revitalized industrial buildings and historic homes, it's a vibrant district full of eclectic shops, restaurants, and breweries. A walking tour of the area is a fantastic way to experience its rich history.

The Sundae's Sweet Start!

In 1881 the first ice cream sundae was created in Two Rivers. Talk about a delicious piece of history! Today, Wisconsinites sure love their ice cream - consuming nearly 21 million gallons each year.

Adventure 238: Learn About the Fur Trade at Fort Crawford Museum

In Prairie du Chien, the Fort Crawford Museum (717 S Beaumont Rd, Prairie du Chien, WI 53821) explores the history of the fort and its role in the fur trade and the Black Hawk War. The exhibits also delve into the history of healthcare, highlighting Dr. William Beaumont's groundbreaking digestive system research conducted at the fort.

Adventure 239: Dig into Mining History at the Platteville Mining Museum

The Platteville Mining Museum (405 E Main St, Platteville, WI 53818) provides a deep dive into the history of lead and zinc mining in Wisconsin. Walk through an authentic 1845 lead mine, view mineral specimens, and learn about the miners who risked their lives to extract the valuable resources.

Adventure 240: Marvel at the Wade House Historic Site

The Wade House Historic Site (W7965 WI-23, Greenbush, WI 53026) transports you back to the 1860s. Explore the beautifully restored Greek Revival style stagecoach inn, enjoy a carriage ride, and explore the fascinating Wesley W. Jung Carriage Museum, showcasing Wisconsin's transportation history.

Adventure 241: Explore Native American Culture at the Neville Public Museum

The Neville Public Museum (210 Museum Pl, Green Bay, WI 54303) features exhibits on art, history, and science, with a special emphasis on Northeast Wisconsin and the Upper Peninsula's cultural heritage. Visit the "On the Edge of the Inland Sea" exhibit to learn about the area's Native American history.

Adventure 242: Fountain City's Rock in the House

Situated in the charming town of Fountain City lies an unexpected historical marvel, the Rock in the House (440 N Shore Dr, Fountain City, WI 54629). This curious attraction came to be in April 1995 when a 55-ton boulder dislodged from a cliff and crashed into the home of Dwight and Maxine Anderson. Luckily, no one was hurt, but the boulder took residence in the house, making the dwelling uninhabitable. Instead of removing the massive stone, the house was sold and converted into a tourist site.

Adventure 243: More Fountain City Fun at Prairie Moon Sculpture Garden

Step into a whimsical world where imagination meets reality at the Prairie Moon Sculpture Garden (52727 Prairie Moon Rd, Fountain City, WI 54629) - just down the road from the Rock in the House which is also in Fountain City. The garden is the extraordinary creation of Herman Rusch, a local farmer, who, after retiring, dedicated his life to the arts, constructing one of the state's most remarkable roadside attractions. His playground of creativity sprawls across an expanse of prairie and hosts a multitude of sculptures built from recycled materials, concrete, and glass.

Adventure 244: Experience Victorian Era at the Villa Louis

Villa Louis Historic Site (521 N Villa Louis Rd, Prairie du Chien, WI 53821) is a beautifully preserved Victorian mansion, once the home of Hercules Dousman, a wealthy frontier entrepreneur. Guided tours provide a glimpse into the lifestyle of the Victorian era with its elegantly furnished rooms and beautifully manicured grounds.

Adventure 245: Step Back in Time at the Castlerock Museum

Unraveling the tapestry of European medieval and Renaissance history, the Castlerock Museum (402 S Second St, Alma, WI 54610) stands as a singularly unique treasure trove of ancient armor and weaponry. This isn't just a museum; it's a time capsule that transports you back to the age of chivalry and knights, with an awe-inspiring collection displayed in a castle-like building that enhances the sense of stepping back in time. Each artifact, from the gleaming suits of armor to the intricate crossbows and swords, tells a riveting story about the people who wielded them and the battles they fought.

Adventure 246: Uncover Ancient Mysteries at the Manitowoc County Historical Society

Located in Manitowoc, the Manitowoc County Historical Society and Pinecrest Historical Village (924 Pine Crest Ln, Manitowoc, WI 54220) features a wide variety of exhibits and historical buildings. Discover the area's rich Native American history, the influence of European settlers, and the development of the local industry and farming.

Adventure 247: Walk in the Footsteps of Pioneers at the Pioneer Village Historical Museum

The Pioneer Village Historical Museum (1866 13 1/2 14th Ave, Cameron, WI 54822) offers visitors a chance to step back in time. This 40-acre museum features more than 30 historical buildings, including a one-room schoolhouse, a blacksmith shop, a log cabin, and a country church.

Adventure 248: Visit the Historic Brewery at Best Place at the Historic Pabst Brewery

In Milwaukee, the Best Place at the Historic Pabst Brewery (917 W Juneau Ave, Milwaukee, WI 53233) offers an opportunity to explore the history of Pabst and the beer industry in Wisconsin. You can tour the beautifully preserved 1858 brewery, learn about the process of beer-making, and even sample some of the brewery's iconic beers.

Adventure 249: Explore the Civil War Era at Camp Randall

In Madison, Camp Randall is a historic military site that was used as a training facility for Union troops during the Civil War. Today, it houses the Wisconsin Veterans Museum (30 W Mifflin St, Madison, WI 53703), offering a chance to learn about the state's military history through interactive exhibits and artifacts.

Adventure 250: Dive into Industrial History at Hamilton Wood Type & Printing Museum

The Hamilton Wood Type & Printing Museum (1816 10th St, Two Rivers, WI 54241) is the only museum dedicated to the preservation, study, production, and printing of wood type. The museum features a vast collection of type and hosts demonstrations and workshops where visitors can learn about traditional printing techniques.

Chapter 17

Educational Adventures

Wisconsin, a state brimming with natural beauty, diverse culture, and rich history, also offers a plethora of opportunities for educational exploration. From immersive learning experiences at museums, science centers, and art galleries to discovering local flora and fauna in nature reserves, there is an educational adventure to suit every interest. This chapter will guide you through unique learning experiences across the state, each offering a chance to dive deeper into Wisconsin's vibrant heritage, scientific wonders, and artistic treasures.

Adventure 251: Explore Ice Age Wonders at the Chippewa Moraine Ice Age Reserve

The Chippewa Moraine Ice Age Reserve (13394 Co Hwy M, New Auburn, WI 54757) offers an excellent opportunity to learn about the Ice Age and its impact on Wisconsin's geography. The David R. Obey Ice Age Interpretive Center features engaging exhibits on glacial history and the wildlife of the era.

Adventure 252: Delve into the World of Physics at the Wisconsin Science Museum

The Wisconsin Science Museum (2300 S Park St, Madison, WI 53713), with its interactive exhibits and live demonstrations, offers an exciting exploration of physics, engineering, and the role of Wisconsin's scientists in global innovation.

Adventure 253: Discover Artistic Techniques at the Leigh Yawkey Woodson Art Museum

Located in Wausau, the Leigh Yawkey Woodson Art Museum (700 N 12th St, Wausau, WI 54403) is renowned for its exhibits dedicated to painting, sculpture, and graphics. Visitors can learn about various artistic techniques and participate in interactive workshops.

Adventure 254: Explore Agricultural History at the Farm Wisconsin Discovery Center Center

This center in Manitowoc County offers a deep dive into Wisconsin's agricultural history and the role of farming in today's society. Interactive exhibits, guided tours of a working dairy farm, and a 4D movie experience provide a comprehensive learning experience. The Farm Wisconsin Discovery Center is located at: 7001 Gass Lake Rd, Manitowoc, WI 54220.

Adventure 255: Learn About Space and Astronomy at the Barlow Planetarium

Situated at the University of Wisconsin-Oshkosh, Fox Cities Campus, the Barlow Planetarium (1478 Midway Rd, Menasha, WI 54952) offers a thrilling journey into the mysteries of the universe. Through spectacular astronomical shows and educational programs, visitors can explore the stars, planets, and galaxies.

Adventure 256: Walk through Geological History at the Chippewa Valley Museum

Located in Carson Park, the Chippewa Valley Museum (1204 E Half Moon Dr, Eau Claire, WI 54703) offers fascinating insights into the geological history of Wisconsin. Visitors can explore a wide array of exhibits, including artifacts from ancient glacial periods and a geology lab with hands-on activities.

Adventure 257: Dive into Natural History at the University of Wisconsin Geology Museum

This museum, located in the University of Wisconsin-Madison, presents a journey through time, featuring fossil collections, mineral displays, and geological exhibits. Visitors can discover ancient sea creatures, dinosaurs, and Wisconsin's glacial past. The Geology Museum is located at: 1215 W Dayton St, Madison, WI 53706.

Adventure 258: Explore Wisconsin's Cultural Heritage at the Waupun Heritage Museum

The Waupun Heritage Museum (22 S Madison St, Waupun, WI 53963) preserves and showcases the cultural heritage of Waupun and surrounding areas. Exhibits cover a range of topics from local industry to folk art, offering an engaging snapshot of the region's history.

Adventure 259: Experience STEM Learning at the Green Bay Fear Haunted House

Although a haunted house, Green Bay Fear Haunted House (1950 Bond St, Green Bay, WI 54303) offers a unique learning opportunity. By leveraging the concept of fear, the attraction introduces visitors to science, technology, engineering, and math (STEM) principles.

Adventure 260: Understand Meteorological Phenomena at the National Weather Service's Milwaukee Office

The National Weather Service's office near Milwaukee (N3533 Hardscrabble Rd, Dousman, WI 53118) offers guided tours that provide a glimpse into the science behind weather predictions and the tools meteorologists use.

Pink Flamingos?

Madison, Wisconsin, has a unique official bird: the pink plastic flamingo. This quirky choice stems from a 1979 prank where University of Wisconsin-Madison students placed 1,008 plastic flamingos on a lawn.

Adventure 261: Explore Wisconsin's Wildlife at the Raptor Education Group

The Raptor Education Group (N2160 W Rollwood Rd, Antigo, WI 54409) provides a unique opportunity to learn about Wisconsin's birds of prey. The center rescues, rehabilitates, and releases these birds, educating visitors on the importance of conservation.

Adventure 262: Experience Wisconsin's Culinary History at the Osthoff Resort's L'ecole de la Maison Cooking School

In Elkhart Lake, visitors can immerse themselves in Wisconsin's culinary traditions at L'ecole de la Maison. The cooking school offers classes covering a variety of Wisconsin's culinary delights. This fun trade school is located at: 101 Osthoff Ave, Elkhart Lake, WI 53020.

Adventure 263: Learn about Folklore at Old School Arts

The Old School Arts and Learning Center (315 S Oneida Ave, Rhinelander, WI 54501) is a treasure trove of folklore and traditional crafts. Workshops teach visitors everything from storytelling to basket weaving.

Adventure 264: Investigate Archaeological Finds at the Logan Museum of Anthropology

Located in Beloit College, the Logan Museum of Anthroplogy (700 College St, Beloit, WI 53511) houses collections from around the world and offers a deeper understanding of human cultural history, including exhibits featuring artifacts from local archaeological excavations.

Adventure 265: Discover Sustainable Farming at the Michael Fields Agricultural Institute

The Michael Fields Agricultural Institute (N8030 Townline Rd, East Troy, WI 53120) promotes sustainable farming practices through research, education, and policy. Visitors can explore the organic farm, attend workshops, and learn about sustainable agriculture.

Adventure 266: Explore Wisconsin's Native Flora at the University of Wisconsin-Madison Arboretum

The University of Wisconsin-Madison Arboretum (1207 Seminole Hwy, Madison, WI 53711) is home to a diverse collection of native plants and offers educational programs on Wisconsin's ecosystems and plant species.

Adventure 267: Learn About Renewable Energy at the Midwest Renewable Energy Association

The Midwest Renewable Energy Association (7558 Deer Rd, Custer, WI 54423) offers tours and workshops on renewable energy technologies, promoting sustainable living.

Adventure 268: Understand the Importance of Watersheds at the Fox-Wolf Watershed Alliance

The Fox-Wolf Watershed Alliance (526 W Wisconsin Ave Suite 2E, Appleton, WI 54911) offers educational programs on the importance of watersheds and the role they play in maintaining healthy ecosystems.

Adventure 269: Study Aquatic Life at the University of Wisconsin's Sea Grant Institute

This institute in Madison conducts research on the Great Lakes and other water resources. Visitors can learn about aquatic ecosystems, water quality, and the importance of conservation. The Sea Grant Institutue is located at: 1975 Willow Dr, Madison, WI 53706.

Adventure 270: Discover Horticulture at the University of Wisconsin's West Madison Agricultural Research Station

The West Madison Agricultural Research Station (8502 Mineral Point Rd, Verona, WI 53593) offers tours and workshops on horticulture, providing an insight into plant breeding, cultivation, and the importance of sustainable farming practices.

Adventure 271: Explore Dairy Science at the University of Wisconsin's Dairy Cattle Center

The University of Wisconsin's Dairy Cattle Center (1815 Linden Dr, Madison, WI 53706) offers a chance to learn about Wisconsin's dairy industry, from cow nutrition to milk processing.

Adventure 272: Learn About Wisconsin's Forests at the Forest Exploration Center

The Forest Exploration Center (1800 Forest Exploration Dr, Wauwatosa, WI 53226) provides hands-on education about Wisconsin's forests, including tree identification, the importance of forests in our ecosystem, and sustainable forestry practices.

Adventure 273: Explore Wisconsin's Geology at the Wisconsin Geological and Natural History Survey

The Wisconsin Geological Survey (3817 Mineral Point Rd, Madison, WI 53705) offers educational resources and research on Wisconsin's geology, groundwater, and minerals.

Chapter 18

Why Is Wisconsin So Drunk? You Asked, We Answered!

Wisconsin's love affair with alcohol dates back to the 19th century when German immigrants brought their brewing traditions to the state. They set up shop in Milwaukee, which quickly became known as the "Beer Capital of the World." Today, Wisconsin is home to some of the biggest names in beer, like Miller and Pabst.

But it's not just about beer! Wisconsin is also famous for its supper clubs, where you can enjoy a classic Old Fashioned cocktail before diving into a hearty meal. And let's not forget about the state's signature drink: the Brandy Old Fashioned. This sweet and boozy concoction is a staple at weddings, holidays, and pretty much any gathering of Cheeseheads.

So, what can you expect if you find yourself in Wisconsin? Well, for starters, you'll probably be offered a drink (or three) within minutes of arriving. Wisconsinites are known for their friendly and welcoming nature, and that often involves sharing a cold one with new friends.

You'll also find that drinking is a big part of the social scene in Wisconsin. From tailgating at Packers games to sipping on Bloody Marys at brunch, there's always an excuse to raise a glass. And if you're looking for a wild night out, you can't go wrong with a visit to one of the state's many bars or breweries.

Of course, it's important to remember to drink responsibly and never drive under the influence. Wisconsin may have a reputation for being a party state, but safety should always come first. Whether you're a beer lover, a cocktail connoisseur, or just looking for a good time, you'll find plenty of opportunities to wet your whistle in the Badger State. Cheers!

Chapter 19

Retreats and Wellness Adventures

Relaxation and wellness, often overlooked amid the hustle and bustle of modern life, are essential elements of any worthwhile journey. In Wisconsin, an array of tranquil retreats and wellness adventures await, offering an opportunity to unwind and rejuvenate amidst nature's magnificence. Away from the more traveled paths, this chapter uncovers a range of unique wellness-focused experiences that encapsulate the spirit of rejuvenation, exploration, and the joy of discovery.

Adventure 274: Practice Mindful Yoga in Kenosha

This serene facility offers a variety of classes for all levels, helping visitors achieve a state of harmony between body and mind. Mindful Yoga Studio (3609 Roosevelt Rd, Kenosha, WI 53142) is a gentle space to practice mindfulness, conscious living, and inner peace, allowing you to dive deeper into the world of holistic well-being.

Adventure 275: Indulge in the Wellness Retreat at Kettle Moraine's YogaLoft

This peaceful sanctuary located amidst scenic views provides the perfect setting to de-stress and reconnect with yourself. Yoga Loft (4927 N Lydell Ave, Glendale, WI 53217) offers classes in multiple yoga styles, meditation sessions, and wellness workshops that promote emotional, mental, and physical health.

Adventure 276: Collect Memories with a Sustainable Souvenir Hunt

During your ecotourism trip, embark on a creative and free activity that promotes sustainability: a Sustainable Souvenir Hunt. Challenge yourself to find unique and meaningful "souvenirs" that leave no negative impact on the environment. Instead of purchasing traditional trinkets, seek out natural treasures like seashells, fallen leaves, or smooth stones that catch your eye. These eco-friendly mementos not only connect you with the destination but also serve as reminders of the beauty and fragility of the natural world. By opting for sustainable souvenirs, you can cherish your memories without leaving a trace and contribute to the preservation of the environment you're exploring.

Adventure 277: Embark on an Immersive Wellness Journey

Known for its all-inclusive wellness programs, retreats at Grand Geneva Resort and Spa (7036 Grand Geneva Way, Lake Geneva, WI 53147) combine fitness activities, nutritious meals, wellness coaching, and spa treatments, providing a comprehensive approach to health and well-being.

Adventure 278: Capture Beauty with a Nature Photography Challenge

Engage in a nature photography challenge during your ecotourism trip to promote sustainability for free. Set a goal to capture captivating images of the local flora, fauna, and scenic landscapes. Use your smartphone or camera to document the beauty around you while being mindful of your surroundings and leaving no trace. Share your photographs on social media or create an online album to spread awareness about the importance of conservation and sustainable tourism practices. Through your stunning visuals, you can inspire others to appreciate and protect the natural wonders you've encountered, fostering a deeper connection to the environment and encouraging sustainable behaviors.

Adventure 279: Explore the Wellness Center in Wausau

The Wausau Wellness Center (512 S 17th Ave, Wausau, WI 54401) is a holistic wellness hub offering therapies like acupuncture, reflexology, and traditional Chinese medicine. Workshops on wellness and holistic healing provide a more profound understanding of holistic health.

Adventure 280: Experience the Calming Ambiance of Spa BenMarNicos

This wellness haven provides a range of spa therapies, from traditional massages and facials to innovative treatments such as lemongrass exfoliation. Spa BenMarNicos is located at: 300 W College Ave, Appleton, WI 54911.

Adventure 281: Plant a Seed of Sustainability

As part of your ecotourism trip, engage in guerrilla gardening to contribute to sustainability for free. Carry a few native seeds or seedlings with you and seek out areas in need of a green touch. Whether it's a neglected patch of land, an urban space, or even a barren roadside, discreetly plant the seeds or seedlings, taking care not to disturb existing ecosystems. By greening these spaces, you not only enhance their visual appeal but also promote biodiversity and contribute to air purification. This act of guerrilla gardening can inspire others to take similar steps towards sustainability, fostering a greener and more eco-conscious environment for all.

Adventure 282: Visit Eau Claire's Lotus Spa

Eau Claire's Lotus Spa (4956 Bullis Farm Rd, Eau Claire, WI 54701) is a wellness sanctuary that offers a variety of body treatments, skincare therapies, and wellness workshops. Here, you can enjoy rejuvenating spa therapies while surrounded by serene natural beauty.

Adventure 283: Green Trails Initiative

Create a "Green Trails Initiative" where your fellow ecotourists can participate in a tree-planting program along popular hiking trails in Wisconsin, promoting reforestation and sustainable tourism. Provide participants with free saplings, along with instructions on proper planting techniques, empowering them to contribute to the environment's restoration while enjoying their ecotourism experience.

Toilet Paper Pioneers!

Green Bay might surprise you as the "Toilet Paper Capital of the World." It's also Wisconsin's oldest city. Fun fact: it was originally called the "Bay of Stinkers" because of the funky smell of its waters. No, that's not related to the toilet paper!

Adventure 284: Get Balanced at the Zen Den

Enrich your wellness journey at the Zen Den (21415 W Greenfield Ave, New Berlin, WI 53146). They offer a range of wellness practices, including yoga, Tai Chi, Qi Gong, and mindfulness meditation. Additionally, holistic healing services like Reiki, Chakra balancing, and crystal therapy provide an in-depth wellness experience.

Adventure 285: Enjoy the Healing Touch

Experience the rejuvenating therapies at Manitowoc's Healing Touch Spa (2788 Manitowoc Rd, Village of Bellevue, WI 54311). From hot stone massages to Ayurvedic treatments, this spa is an oasis of relaxation and healing in the heart of Wisconsin.

Adventure 286: Visit the Sheboygan Wellness Studio

They offer an integrated approach to wellness with offerings like yoga, meditation, fitness classes, and health coaching. Regular workshops on nutrition, mindfulness, and stress management equip you with tools for a healthier lifestyle. Sheboyan Wellness Studio is located at: 534 S Pier Dr, Sheboygan, WI 53081.

Adventure 287: Meditate in Beautiful Janesville

Explore the wellness offerings at Flow & Co. Wellness Studio (4335 Milton Ave #110, Janesville, WI 53546). Here, you can engage in a variety of wellness practices, including yoga, Pilates, Tai Chi, and guided meditation.

Adventure 288: Unwind at the St. Croix Healing Arts Center

This wellness hub offers a range of therapies, including reiki therapy, massage, acupuncture, chiropractic treatments, and wellness workshops that nourish the body and soul. St. Croix

Healing Arts Center is located at: 411 Co Rd UU #3, Hudson, WI 54016.

Adventure 289: Holistic Wellness Experience in Bayfield

Enjoy a holistic wellness experience at a Wild Rice Retreat (84860 Old San Rd, Bayfield, WI 54814). This retreat provides a comprehensive wellness program that focus on creating space for healing the mind, body and spirit.

Adventure 290: Visit the Kohler Waters Spa at Lodge Kohler

Offering holistic therapies like acupuncture, massage, and energy healing, this center is a haven of well-being and tranquility. Kohler Waters Spa at Lodge Kohler is located at: 1950 S Ridge Rd, Green Bay, WI 54304.

Adventure 291: Unwind, Recharge and Connect with Forest Bathing

Escape the demands of daily life and embark on a transformative wellness journey without breaking the bank. Discover the serene beauty of nature by embracing a free wellness travel idea: forest bathing. Leave behind the bustling city streets and immerse yourself in the calming embrace of lush green forests. As you wander through the enchanting woodland, allow the gentle rustle of leaves and the melodious chirping of birds to wash away stress and rejuvenate your soul. Inhale the refreshing scent of pine and earth, grounding yourself in the present moment. Engage your senses fully as you touch the moss-covered trees, listen to the babbling brooks, and observe the intricate dance of sunlight filtering through the canopy above. With each step, feel the healing energy of nature infuse your being, restoring balance and promoting a profound sense of well-being. Unwind, recharge, and reconnect with yourself amidst the harmonious embrace of the forest—this free wellness travel idea promises a transformative experience that nourishes both mind and body.

Adventure 292: Tranquility in Menomonie

Experience the tranquility at the Woodland Ridge Retreat (E4620 Cty Rd C, Menomonie, WI 54751). A haven for creatives, a retreat here will help you to rejuvenate amidst the beautiful, forested landscape. Perfect getaway for quilting clubs, scrapbookers and fiber artists.

Adventure 293: Get a Massage in Chippewa Falls

Balance focuses on holistic health and well-being through massage therapy. Balance Therapeutic Massage is located in The Garage Salon at 45 E Elm St, Chippewa Falls, WI 54729.

Adventure 294: Discover Inner Peace in Oshkosh

Experience the calming ambiance of Arise Balanced Wellness (1810 Evans St., Oshkosh, 54901). Offering a variety of wellness treatments like yoga, meditation, and wellness coaching, this center allows you to retreat from the stress of daily life and find inner peace.

Adventure 295: Visit the La Crosse Therapeutic Salt Caves

With a tranquil environment that promotes relaxation, this wellness destination provides an incredible retreat for those seeking an alternative wellness experience. Salt Fix Vitality Center is located at: 608 4th St S, La Crosse, WI 54601. They are by appointment only.

Adventure 296: Nature Becomes Your Classroom with Eco-Art

Engage in a free eco-art experience in the beauty of Wisconsin's outdoors. Gather natural materials like fallen leaves, twigs, and pinecones to create beautiful artwork. This activity is especially fun for families with kids as it promotes sustainability by showcasing the beauty of the environment while encouraging participants to leave no trace and appreciate nature's resources.

Chapter 20

Adventures at Art, Film and Music Festivals

The essence of Wisconsin doesn't only lie in its stunning natural attractions or delicious dairy delights; its culture and arts scene is equally enthralling. This chapter encapsulates adventures related to the dynamic and diverse Art, Film, and Music Festivals in Wisconsin, which are pulsating with life, color, and rhythm.

Adventure 297: Driftless Film Festival in Mineral Point

This annual event takes place in the historic Mineral Point, a town known for its artistry and charm. The Driftless Film Festival brings together the best of new indie films, local filmmakers, and students, providing a unique platform for talented voices. You can catch a variety of films, participate in Q&A sessions, and immerse yourself in the vibrant world of cinema.

Adventure 298: Milwaukee Underground Film Festival

Celebrating artists who push the boundaries of cinema, the Milwaukee Underground Film Festival is a student-run, international festival dedicated to showcasing independent, artist-driven cinema. Here, you can discover new voices, watch unconventional narratives, and experience the bold world of indie filmmaking.

Adventure 299: Eau Claire Jazz Festival

This is one of the largest jazz festivals in the country, offering exceptional music performances by talented musicians from all corners of the globe. Over the course of two days, you can enjoy street jazz, college competitions, and top-notch performances from renowned jazz artists.

Adventure 300: Chippewa Valley Rock Festival

One for rock music fans, this outdoor music festival in Cadott features performances by top international rock bands. Along with music, there are opportunities for camping and shopping at various onsite vendors, offering a well-rounded festival experience.

Adventure 301: Mile of Music Festival in Appleton

A diverse mix of original artists converge on downtown Appleton for this annual music festival. The event focuses on up-and-coming musicians and singer-songwriters, spanning a variety of genres and styles, and is a fantastic opportunity to discover new music.

Adventure 302: Green Bay Film Festival

Independent filmmakers from around the world gather to showcase their work at the Green Bay Film Festival. Attendees can enjoy a myriad of films, workshops, discussions, and meet and greets with the filmmakers.

Adventure 303: Woodland Pattern's Annual Poetry Marathon & Benefit

Based in Milwaukee, this day-long event offers a platform for poets from diverse backgrounds to share their works. Attendees can also participate in the open mic session, creating an engaging environment for poetry enthusiasts.

Adventure 304: Lakefront Festival of Art in Milwaukee

Held annually on the grounds of the Milwaukee Art Museum, this festival features works from nearly 200 artists from around the nation. Along with art exhibitions, attendees can enjoy live music, food from local vendors, and interactive art activities.

Adventure 305: Indian Summer Festival in Milwaukee

This annual festival celebrates Native American culture through traditional music, dance, crafts, and food. It's a fantastic opportunity to learn about Wisconsin's indigenous cultures and participate in traditional ceremonies and activities.

Adventure 306: Beloit International Film Festival

Celebrating indie films from around the globe, this film festival offers ten days of film screenings, workshops, and panels. Attendees can expect to see everything from documentaries and shorts to animated and experimental films.

Famous Cheeseheads!

Notable folks from Wisconsin include: Laura Ingalls Wilder, Georgia O'Keeffe, Chris Farley, Mark Ruffalo, Willem Dafoe, and Orson Welles. Harry Houdini was born in Hungary, he spent his childhood in Appleton, Wisconsin.

Adventure 307: Madison World Music Festival

A celebration of music from around the world, this festival features a line-up of international artists performing on outdoor stages. The event also includes workshops and meet-and-greets, providing a rich cultural experience.

Adventure 308: Have a Hodagin' Hootenanny

Prepare for a foot-stomping, soul-lifting experience at the Hodag Country Festival in Rhinelander. Every summer, thousands of country music enthusiasts flock to this remarkable event to celebrate the rich traditions of country music. With a history spanning over 40 years and a lineup featuring the biggest names in the country music scene, this festival is a staple in Wisconsin's cultural calendar. It's a phenomenal gathering that combines the love for music with the joyous spirit of Wisconsin's community. Don't miss out on this essential country music rendezvous in the Badger State.

Adventure 309: Riverwest 24 in Milwaukee

This 24-hour bike race is more of a community event than a competition, with live music, film screenings, and food trucks lining the course. It's a unique blend of sport and culture that showcases the vibrant Riverwest neighborhood.

Adventure 310: Fun for Everyone at the Iola Car Show

Experience the roar of engines and the gleam of chrome at the Iola Car Show, one of the largest auto events in America. This annual spectacle in Iola, Wisconsin showcases over 2,200 show cars, 4,200 swap spaces, 1,000 car corral spaces, and 1,600 camping spaces. It's not just a festival for car enthusiasts; with live music, great food, and fun activities for the entire family, the Iola Car Show offers a delightful celebration of American automotive history that has something for everyone.

Adventure 311: Madison Popfest

This annual music festival focuses on the pop genre, showcasing local and national indie pop acts. With an intimate venue and a friendly, laid-back atmosphere, it's a great way to discover new music.

Adventure 312: Country Thunder in Twin Lakes

For fans of country music, this four-day festival features a line-up of big names and emerging talents in country music. In addition to music, there's also a range of food and merchandise vendors, a camping site, and fun activities to keep everyone entertained.

Adventure 313: Appleton's Octoberfest

A celebration of all things fall, this festival includes live music across multiple stages, hundreds of food and craft vendors, family-friendly activities, and a classic car show.

Adventure 314: African Cultural Festival in Madison

A celebration of African culture, this festival features live music, traditional dance, authentic African cuisine, and arts and crafts. It's a vibrant and interactive way to learn about the diverse cultures of Africa.

Adventure 315: Celebrate the Culture and Spirit of the Driftless Region

Immerse yourself in the melodic landscape of the Driftless Music Festival, a free, annual summer event held in the picturesque region of Viroqua, Wisconsin. Here, you'll find a vibrant mix of music genres, from folk and bluegrass to rock and jazz, that matches the diverse and stunning beauty of the Driftless Area itself. Alongside the music, the festival also features local food vendors and artists, making it a true celebration of the culture and spirit of the Driftless Region.

Adventure 316: Northern Sky Theater in Fish Creek

This professional theater company presents original, family-friendly musicals at the Peninsula State Park Amphitheater (10169 Shore Rd., Fish Creek, WI 54212). It's a magical experience to watch a show amid the lush beauty of the Northwoods.

Adventure 317: Chalk Fest in Wausau

This two-day street art festival turns the city's sidewalks into colorful murals. Artists from around the nation participate, transforming the downtown area into a vibrant outdoor gallery.

Adventure 318: Experience the Culinary Delights of Jewish Food

Experience the culinary delights of the Jewish Food Festival in Mequon, Wisconsin. This annual festival offers attendees a delicious chance to sample traditional Jewish foods, including matzo ball soup, challah, and an array of kosher deli items. Moreover, you'll get to participate in baking workshops, watch cooking demos, and learn about the rich cultural and historical contexts behind these beloved dishes. So, bring your appetite and join in the celebration of Jewish cuisine in the heart of the Badger State!

Adventure 319: Experimental Aircraft Association (EAA) AirVenture in Oshkosh

While technically not an art, film, or music festival, this week-long event is a celebration of aviation and aeronautical innovations, featuring daily airshows, workshops, and demonstrations. The festival also showcases aircraft from various eras, from vintage planes to futuristic prototypes, attracting aviation enthusiasts from around the world.

Chapter 21

Sustainable Adventures

As we continue our journey through Wisconsin, we will discover new realms of natural beauty and exhilarating adventure that coexist harmoniously with their surroundings. In this chapter, we delve into a set of extraordinary experiences that balance the excitement of discovery with a respectful, sustainable approach to the environment. Let us embark on sustainable adventures that take us from pristine waters to towering forests, from dynamic cities to charming small towns, and all places in between.

Adventure 320: Kayaking on the Wisconsin River

One of the best ways to enjoy Wisconsin's scenic waterways in a sustainable way is through kayaking. Paddle your way along the Wisconsin River, taking in the surrounding landscape and abundant wildlife. With the soothing sound of water lapping against your boat and the sight of eagles soaring overhead, you'll find peace, adventure, and a profound respect for Wisconsin's natural beauty.

Adventure 321: Wildflower Hiking in Prairie du Chien

This area is well-known for its sprawling meadows of colorful wildflowers. Guided hikes provide you with an up-close and personal view of this natural phenomenon, while educating you about the importance of protecting these delicate ecosystems.

Adventure 322: Birdwatching at Necedah National Wildlife Refuge

The Necedah National Wildlife Refuge (N11385 Headquarters Rd, Necedah, WI 54646) is a paradise for bird lovers. It's home to over 200 bird species including endangered whooping cranes. The quiet tranquility of the refuge and the rare opportunity to see these incredible creatures make this a must-do adventure.

Adventure 323: Biking in Dodgeville

Discover the rolling hills and picturesque farmland of Wisconsin's heartland on a bike tour of Dodgeville. The town's sustainable ethos is reflected in its cycling culture, with numerous bike paths allowing you to explore the region while minimizing your carbon footprint.

Adventure 324: Farmer's Market in Waunakee

Get a taste of Wisconsin's bounty at this lively farmer's market located at the Waun-A-Bowl parking lot (301 S Century Ave, Waunakee, WI 53597). Featuring local farmers and artisans, it's the perfect place to sample organic produce and handcrafted goods, all while supporting the local economy and sustainable farming practices.

Adventure 325: Volunteering at Wild Instincts in Rhinelander

Wild Instincts (4621 Apperson Dr, Rhinelander, WI 54501) is a wildlife rehabilitation center which offers a unique opportunity to learn about and contribute to the protection of Wisconsin's native wildlife. Participate in their volunteer programs, which range from helping injured animals to habitat restoration.

Adventure 326: Canoeing at the Brule River State Forest

Brule River State Forest (6250 Ranger Rd, Brule, WI 54820) offers 50 miles of canoeing and kayaking trails that run through dense forests and serene wetlands. It's a peaceful, low-impact way to immerse yourself in nature and explore the beauty of Wisconsin's wilderness.

Adventure 327: Sustainable Wine Tour in Viroqua

This town is home to several wineries committed to organic and sustainable viticulture. Embark on a wine tour to sample their wines, learn about their green practices, and explore their picturesque vineyards.

Adventure 328: Solar Farm Visit in Jefferson

Learn about renewable energy at one of Wisconsin's largest solar farms. Guided tours offer fascinating insights into how sunlight is transformed into electricity, showcasing Wisconsin's commitment to a sustainable future.

Adventure 329: Organic Dairy Farming in Kewaunee County

Visit a local organic dairy farm to learn about sustainable farming practices. Participate in farm activities and taste the difference that organic, ethically-raised dairy makes.

A Tasty Law!

Between 1935 and 1937, Wisconsin had a law requiring all restaurants to serve cheese and butter with every meal.

Adventure 330: Travel Light and Leave No Trace

Embrace the philosophy of 'Travel Light, Leave No Trace' on your Wisconsin adventures. This involves making decisions that minimize your impact on the environment, promoting sustainability while still fully experiencing all that Wisconsin has to offer. Pack only what you need, reducing unnecessary waste, and always dispose of your trash properly, utilizing recycling facilities whenever possible. Make use of refillable water bottles and eco-friendly toiletries. When exploring Wisconsin's stunning natural parks, stick to the marked trails, and never disturb wildlife or plant life. Remember, you're a guest in their home. By choosing to 'Travel Light, Leave No Trace', you can ensure that Wisconsin's beauty is preserved for future generations to enjoy.

Adventure 331: Renewable Energy Tour in Eau Claire

Explore the world of renewable energy with a guided tour through Eau Claire's wind farms and hydroelectric power plants. This adventure offers a look into how the state generates green power and the efforts to make Wisconsin more sustainable.

Adventure 332: Local Artisan Workshops in Bayfield

Get hands-on experience with sustainable crafting in the local artisan workshops in Bayfield. From pottery to woodworking, learn a new skill and create a unique, handmade memento of your Wisconsin adventures.

Adventure 333: Sailing on Lake Superior

Set sail on the crystal clear waters of Lake Superior. This wind-powered adventure gives you the opportunity to explore the lake's numerous islands and marvel at its scenic shoreline.

Adventure 334: Adopt-a-Trail Program

Search for an Adopt-a-Trail program where ecotourists can volunteer their time to maintain and preserve hiking trails in Wisconsin. Participants can choose a trail, commit to regular cleanups, trail maintenance, and removal of invasive species, fostering a sense of ownership and responsibility for the environment. This initiative promotes sustainable ecotourism and ensures the long-term preservation of Wisconsin's natural beauty.

Adventure 335: Visit a Local Farm in Fond du Lac

Spend a day at a local farm in Fond du Lac, getting up close with animals, learning about sustainable farming practices, and tasting fresh, farm-to-table foods.

Adventure 336: Eco-Friendly Brewery Tours in New Glarus

Sample delicious, sustainably-brewed beer at the eco-friendly breweries of New Glarus. Learn about the brewing process and how these breweries are making a positive environmental impact.

Adventure 337: Sustainable Shopping in Port Washington

Take part in the local economy and shop sustainably by visiting the town's many stores that specialize in locally-made, eco-friendly products.

Adventure 338: Visit the Waupaca Eco Park

Explore Waupaca's innovative Eco Park (Webster Way, Waupaca, WI 54981). It's a perfect place for outdoor activities like hiking and bird watching, and it's also home to a variety of renewable energy and water conservation demonstrations.

Adventure 339: Consider Eco-Friendly Transportation

Wisconsin offers various eco-friendly transportation options for the environmentally conscious traveler. Make use of public transit systems, such as buses and trains, which significantly reduce the carbon footprint compared to private vehicles. Additionally, many Wisconsin cities, including Madison and Milwaukee, have robust bike-sharing programs.

Biking is not only a sustainable mode of transport, but it also allows for a more intimate exploration of the cities' scenic paths and trails. In rural areas, consider carpooling or using electric car rental services, which are becoming increasingly prevalent. When exploring Wisconsin's beautiful outdoors, consider hiking or canoeing, activities that have minimal environmental impact. By prioritizing eco-friendly transportation, you can contribute to preserving Wisconsin's environment while having an unforgettable adventure.

Adventure 340: Explore the Eco-Friendly Architecture in Stevens Point

Tour the green buildings of Stevens Point, exploring the innovations in sustainable architecture and design that make the city an eco-friendly urban haven.

Adventure 341: Learn about Composting in Appleton

Visit a local composting facility in Appleton to learn how food and yard waste can be turned into nutrient-rich soil, an important step towards sustainable waste management.

Adventure 342: Visit the Renewable Energy Research Center in Platteville

Take a tour of this cutting-edge facility to learn about the latest advancements in renewable energy technology and their potential for creating a more sustainable future.

<h1 align="center">Chapter 22</h1>

<h1 align="center">Adventures at Quirky Roadside
Attractions</h1>

There's a strange but intriguing beauty to be found along the backroads and byways of any region. Often, they're full of quirky, often overlooked attractions that hold a charm of their own. This chapter will detail adventures showcasing the whimsy and local flavor of our selection of quirky roadside attractions. Each of these adventures promises a unique experience that veers off the beaten track, presenting you with sights that are truly one of a kind.

Adventure 343: Bessie the Cow in Janesville

Located in Janesville, Bessie the Cow (3511-3507, WI-26 Trunk, Janesville, WI 53545) is a gigantic fiberglass statue standing guard over the Pine Tree Plaza. Perfect for an unusual photo op, Bessie is a tribute to Wisconsin's dairy industry.

Adventure 344: Jurustic Park in Marshfield

Jurustic Park (112021 Old Sugar Bush Ln, Marshfield, WI 54449) is a delightful blend of creativity and humor. Here, you'll find a collection of whimsical, rusted metal sculptures depicting creatures said to have roamed the Marshfield area during the Iron Age.

Adventure 345: Sputnik Crash Site in Manitowoc

A cast bronze ring and marker in the middle of the street in Manitowoc commemorate the site where a 20-pound piece of Sputnik IV crashed in 1962. This quirky attraction is a nod to a unique moment in history. Find the Sputnik Crash Site at 798 Park St, Manitowoc, WI 54220.

Adventure 346: Fred Smith's Concrete Park in Phillips

Fred Smith's Concrete Park (N8236 State Hwy 13, Phillips, WI 54555) is a fascinating collection of over 200 concrete and glass sculptures created by Fred Smith, a self-taught artist. From political figures to mythical creatures, these sculptures are a testament to one man's artistic vision.

Adventure 347: The World's Largest Talking Cow in Neillsville

Chatty Belle (1200 E Division St, Neillsville, WI 54456), is a beloved and iconic attraction that holds a special place in the hearts of locals and visitors alike. Known as the "World's

Largest Talking Cow," Chatty Belle is a larger-than-life fiberglass sculpture of a Holstein cow, standing proudly in a picturesque field. Chatty Belle's unique feature lies in her ability to "talk" when activated by visitors, providing a fun and interactive experience. With a press of a button, visitors can hear fascinating tidbits about cows, farming, and the rich agricultural heritage of the area.

Adventure 348: Dr. Evermor's Forevertron Sculpture Park in North Freedom

At Dr. Evermor's Forevertron (S7703 US-12, North Freedom, WI 53951), you can explore an array of fascinating kinetic sculptures and mythical creatures made of scrap metal, all designed by the talented Tom Every.

Adventure 349: Mustard Museum in Middleton

The eccentric National Mustard Museum (7477 Hubbard Ave, Middleton, WI 53562) houses a collection of more than 6,000 mustards from all over the world and pays tribute to the history of this beloved condiment.

Adventure 350: The Dickeyville Grotto and Shrines

The Dickeyville Grotto and Shrines (255-377 Great River Rd, Dickeyville, WI 53808) is a beautiful roadside attraction which showcases intricate religious and patriotic-themed grottoes and gardens built by Father Matthias Wernerus, a local Catholic priest.

Adventure 351: World's Largest Six-Pack in La Crosse

In La Crosse, you'll find the World's Largest Six-Pack (3rd St S, La Crosse, WI 54601) - a collection of six huge storage tanks painted to resemble a six-pack of beer, a tribute to the city's brewing history.

Adventure 352: Ben Bikin' in Sparta

Sparta, the self-proclaimed "Bicycling Capital of America," pays tribute to this title with Ben Bikin', a towering statue of a Victorian gentleman on a penny-farthing bicycle. Visit the Ben Bikin' sculpture at: 101 E Wisconsin St, Sparta, WI 54656.

America's Dairyland!

Wisconsin produces the most cheese and the second highest amount of milk in the U.S., earning nicknames like "The Dairy State" and "The Cheese State." Also, the town of Monroe is known as the "Swiss Cheese Capital of the World."

Adventure 353: The Hodag in Rhinelander

Head to Rhinelander to see the Hodag, a mythical creature that is the official symbol of the city. A statue of this creature, which has the head of a frog, the back of a dinosaur, and the tail of a speckled fish, sits outside the Rhinelander Area

Chamber of Commerce (450 W Kemp St, Rhinelander, WI 54501).

Adventure 354: Go Swingin' at the Swing Park

Under the shadow of Milwaukee's Holton Street Bridge (1733-1739 N Water St, Milwaukee, WI 53212), you'll find an unexpected treat: the Swing Park. This public space takes advantage of the structure's underbelly, transforming it into an urban playground. With various swings hanging from the bridge itself, it adds an element of fun and whimsy to the cityscape. As you swing, take a moment to appreciate the blend of urban architecture and playful creativity that defines this unique Wisconsin attraction.

Adventure 355: Freshwater Fishing Hall of Fame in Hayward

This museum in Hayward, which celebrates freshwater fishing, is most notable for the "Shrine to Anglers," a gigantic four-and-a-half story musky fish that you can climb inside for a great view of the surroundings. Visit the Freshwater Fishing Hall of Fame at: 10360 Hall of Fame Dr, Hayward, WI 54843.

Adventure 356: Deke Slayton Space and Bicycle Museum in Sparta

In Sparta, you'll find an unusual combination of interests housed under one roof: the Deke Slayton Space and Bicycle Museum (200 W Main St, Sparta, WI 54656), where you can learn about astronaut Deke Slayton's life and the history of bicycles.

Adventure 357: Tommy Bartlett Exploratory in Wisconsin Dells

Filled with hands-on science exhibits, the Tommy Bartlett Exploratory (560 Wisconsin Dells Pkwy, Wisconsin Dells, WI 53965) offers unique entertainment, including a replica of the Russian Space Station Mir.

Adventure 358: FAST Corporation in Sparta

The FAST Corporation's Fiberglass Mold Graveyard (14177 Co Hwy Q, Sparta, WI 54656) is an open field filled with molds and damaged statues. The eerie spectacle is oddly fascinating, with decaying, oversized fiberglass creatures from across the decades.

Adventure 359: Gile's Flowage in Hurley

Gile's Flowage in Hurley is a man-made body of water, known for the stunning reflections of the surrounding landscape on its surface. On a calm day, it's hard to tell where the sky ends and the water begins.

Adventure 360: Victorian Chocolate Shoppe in Sheboygan

The Victorian Chocolate Shoppe (519 S 8th St, Sheboygan, WI 53081) is a delightful step back in time, with vintage candy and soda, antique fixtures, and old-fashioned customer service.

Adventure 361: Selfies at the Seeds of Hope

In Eau Claire, you can find an entire farm filled with sunflowers. Babbette's Seeds of Hope (S5875 Fuller Rd, Eau Claire, WI 54701) is a beautiful, sprawling field of golden blooms that provides a great photo opportunity and a relaxing, cheerful atmosphere.

Adventure 362: Step Back in Time at Elmer's Auto and Toy Museum

Step back in time at Elmer's Auto and Toy Museum (W903 Elmers Rd, Fountain City, WI 54629). A treasure trove for all ages, Elmer's features an impressive collection of classic cars, thousands of antique toys, and numerous nostalgic artifacts. Stroll among vintage bicycles, pedal cars, and dolls, and marvel at beautifully restored classic cars. As you navigate through the museum nestled on a picturesque hillside, it's a trip down memory lane and a fun-filled educational experience all rolled into one.

Adventure 363: World's Largest Penny in Woodruff

In Woodruff, you'll find the World's Largest Penny (820 3rd Ave, Woodruff, WI 54568), a concrete monument built in the 1950s to commemorate a successful local fundraising campaign.

Adventure 364: Bristol Renaissance Faire in Kenosha

Take a step back in time at the Bristol Renaissance Faire (12550 120th Ave, Kenosha, WI 53142), where you can enjoy a taste of 16th century English life, complete with arts, crafts, games, rides, food, music, and theatrical performances.

Adventure 365: Fennimore Doll and Toy Museum

In Fennimore, you'll find a museum dedicated to the simpler joys of childhood. The Fennimore Doll and Toy Museum (1135 6th St, Fennimore, WI 53809) features dolls, toys, and miniatures dating back to the 1700s.

Chapter 23

Accommodation Suggestions

Wisconsin is a state with diverse accommodation options catering to every budget and travel style. From budget-friendly hostels to luxurious resorts, you'll find plenty of fantastic places to rest your head at night. For travelers seeking something out of the ordinary, there are also unique stays that offer an experience you won't soon forget. Here are some recommendations based on different travel budgets and preferences.

Budget

- **HI Madison Hostel, Madison:** The HI Madison Hostel (141 S Butler St., Madison, WI 53703) is a fantastic option for travelers on a budget. Located in the heart of Madison, this hostel offers dormitory-style rooms and a communal kitchen, making it a great place to meet fellow travelers. The hostel's central location makes it easy to explore the city's main attractions.

- **Super 8 by Wyndham, Green Bay:** A reliable choice for budget accommodation is the Super 8 by Wyndham (2868 S Oneida St., Green Bay WI 54304). Located near the Green Bay airport, this motel offers clean and comfortable rooms at an affordable price. They provide free Wi-Fi and breakfast, as well as a fitness center.

- **Apostle Islands Area Campground, Bayfield:** For those who prefer an outdoor adventure, the Apostle Islands Area Campground (85150 Trailer Ct, Bayfield, WI 54814) provides a budget-friendly alternative to traditional accommodations. Enjoy the beauty of the Apostle Islands while camping under the stars.

Mid-range

- **The Edgewater Hotel, Madison:** The Edgewater (1001 Wisconsin Pl, Madison, WI 53703) is a historic hotel located in downtown Madison. It offers comfortable rooms with modern amenities, multiple dining options, and a full-service spa. The hotel also boasts stunning views of Lake Mendota.

- **The Brewhouse Inn & Suites, Milwaukee:** Located in the former Pabst Brewery, this boutique hotel combines history with modern comfort. The rooms maintain some of the building's original features, like exposed brick walls and steel beam ceilings, giving it a unique industrial chic vibe. The Brewhouse Inn & Suites is located at: 1215 N 10th St, Milwaukee, WI 53205.

- **CopperLeaf Boutique Hotel & Spa, Appleton:** The CopperLeaf Boutique Hotel & Spa (300 W College Ave, Appleton, WI 54911) is a mid-range option that provides a touch of luxury. It offers beautifully appointed rooms and suites, a full-service spa, and a fine dining restaurant.

Luxury

- **The American Club, Kohler:** For a luxurious stay, consider The American Club (419 Highland Dr, Kohler, WI 53044). This historic hotel offers high-end rooms and suites, a golf course, several restaurants, and the Kohler Waters Spa, one of the most acclaimed spas in the world.
- **The Pfister Hotel, Milwaukee:** The Pfister Hotel (424 E Wisconsin Ave, Milwaukee, WI 53202) is a luxury landmark in Milwaukee. It's known for its stunning Victorian architecture, elegant rooms, world-class dining, and a vast Victorian art collection. The hotel's rooftop lounge offers panoramic city views.

- **Canoe Bay, Chetek:** Canoe Bay (W16065 Hogback Rd, Chetek, WI 54728) is a secluded luxury resort located near Chetek. It offers private cabins on a serene lake, making it the perfect choice for a romantic getaway. The resort also features gourmet dining and various outdoor activities.

Unique Stays

- **Journey Inn, Maiden Rock:** For a unique and holistic retreat, consider the Journey Inn (W3671 200th Ave, Maiden Rock, WI 54750). This eco-retreat offers themed rooms that focus on different elements of nature, daily yoga classes, and a range of therapeutic services, including massage and energy healing.
- **Don Q Inn, Dodgeville:** The Don Q Inn (3658 WI-23, Dodgeville, WI 53533) is an eccentric hotel known for its themed rooms. Whether you stay in the Northern Lights room, complete with an igloo and aurora borealis mural, or the Oriental Gardens room, which features a queen-size bed atop a koi pond, you're guaranteed a memorable experience.
- **Frank Lloyd Wright's Seth Peterson Cottage, Mirror Lake:** Frank Lloyd Wright fans will jump at the chance to stay in the Seth Peterson Cottage (E9982 Fern Dell Rd, Reedsburg, WI 53959). Located in Mirror Lake State Park, this single-room cottage offers guests

a unique opportunity to live within a Wright-designed space.

Whether you're a budget backpacker, a luxury seeker, or a traveler in search of a unique experience, Wisconsin offers a wealth of options to make your stay as enjoyable and memorable as possible.

Chapter 24

Transportation

Navigating Wisconsin is easy thanks to the state's well-developed transportation infrastructure. Whether you choose to travel by air, car, bus, bike, or public transportation, you'll find numerous convenient options at your disposal. Below, we break down the best ways to get around the state.

By Air

- **Milwaukee's General Mitchell International Airport (MKE):** This is the largest airport in Wisconsin, providing numerous domestic and international flights. Located in Milwaukee, it's the gateway to southeastern Wisconsin.
- **Dane County Regional Airport (MSN):** Situated in Madison, this airport offers daily

nonstop flights to several major cities across the country.

- **Green Bay Austin Straubel International Airport (GRB):** For those heading to northeastern Wisconsin, GRB provides direct flights to and from many U.S. hubs.

By Car

Traveling by car offers the most flexibility to explore Wisconsin at your own pace. Interstates I-94, I-90, and I-43 are the primary routes running through the state. Rental cars are widely available at airports and city centers. Remember, Wisconsin has strict laws against drunk driving, and seatbelts are mandatory.

What are the four seasons in Wisconsin? Almost winter, winter, still winter and construction.

By Bus

- **Greyhound:** Greyhound buses connect many

of Wisconsin's major cities, offering an economical way to traverse the state.

- **Badger Bus:** This service provides regular routes between Madison and Milwaukee.
- **Jefferson Lines:** Operating across the Midwest, Jefferson Lines connects Wisconsin to neighboring states.

Public Transportation

Most of Wisconsin's larger cities, like Madison and Milwaukee, have extensive public transportation systems.

- **Milwaukee County Transit System (MCTS):** MCTS operates numerous bus routes throughout Milwaukee County.
- **Madison Metro Transit:** In Madison, the Metro Transit offers comprehensive bus services throughout the city and its suburbs.
- **Green Bay Metro:** For those in Green Bay, the Green Bay Metro provides local bus service.

By Bike

Wisconsin is known for its bike-friendly cities and beautiful trails. Cities like Madison and Milwaukee have numerous bike rental shops and bike-sharing programs. The state also boasts hundreds of miles of scenic bike trails like the Elroy-Sparta State Trail and the Capital City State Trail.

Rideshares and Taxis

Rideshare services like Uber and Lyft are widely available in Wisconsin's larger cities and towns. Traditional taxi services also operate throughout the state, with numerous local companies in each city.

From convenient air travel to scenic bike paths, Wisconsin's diverse range of transportation options make it easy to get around and explore all the fantastic sights this state has to offer. No matter your preference, there's a mode of transportation that will suit your needs.

Chapter 25

Local Cuisine

O ne of the highlights of any trip to Wisconsin is undoubtedly the food. Known for its dairy products, particularly cheese, Wisconsin has a food scene that's rich in tradition, with a new wave of culinary innovation adding exciting dimensions to the state's gastronomic landscape. Below, we explore some must-try dishes and the best places to enjoy a meal.

Must-try Dishes

- **Cheese Curds:** When you're in America's Dairyland, trying cheese curds is a must. These nuggets of deep-fried or fresh cheese are a Wisconsin staple. For an authentic experience, try them at a local dairy or cheese factory.
- **Bratwurst:** Brought to the state by German settlers, bratwurst sausages have become a Wisconsin classic. Whether served at a backyard

barbecue or a baseball game, they're best enjoyed grilled and topped with sauerkraut and mustard.
- **Fish Fry:** A tradition especially popular during the Lenten season, but enjoyed year-round, the Friday night fish fry is an event in itself. Locally caught fish, usually perch, bluegill, or walleye, is beer-battered and deep-fried, and served with sides like coleslaw, rye bread, and tartar sauce.

Notable Restaurants

- **L'Etoile, Madison:** This farm-to-table restaurant has been a pillar of Madison's dining scene for decades. Chef Tory Miller's focus on local, seasonal ingredients shines through in dishes that are innovative, flavorful, and quintessentially Wisconsin. L'Etoile Restaurant is located at: 1 S Pinckney St, Madison, WI 53703.
- **Sanford, Milwaukee:** One of the state's most critically acclaimed restaurants, Sanford (1547

N Jackson St, Milwaukee, WI 53202) serves up a daily changing menu filled with creative dishes inspired by the culinary traditions of Wisconsin and beyond.

- **Farm Table, Amery:** Located in a restored historic building in the small town of Amery, Farm Table (110 Keller Ave N, Amery, WI 54001) is a restaurant dedicated to local, organic, and sustainably-produced foods. The menu, which changes seasonally, reflects the best produce and ingredients the region has to offer.

From beer-battered fish fries to award-winning restaurants, Wisconsin's food scene is as diverse as it is delicious. Whether you're a food connoisseur or simply someone who enjoys a good meal, the Badger State has a culinary experience for you.

Chapter 26

Additional Resources

Beyond the stunning landscapes, delicious food, and warm hospitality, it's important for every traveler to have essential information on hand. This chapter provides resources that could be useful in an emergency, as well as apps and websites to make your Wisconsin trip more convenient and enjoyable.

Emergency Numbers

- **Police, Fire, and Medical Emergencies:** Dial 911
- **Non-emergency Police Service:** Contact the local police station
- **Roadside Assistance:** Contact the Wisconsin Department of Transportation at (608) 266-2112 for assistance with non-emergency roadside incidents.

Useful Apps

- **Travel Wisconsin:** This official app of the Wisconsin Department of Tourism has travel guides, event listings, articles, and more.
- **OnMilwaukee:** For travelers to Milwaukee, this app provides restaurant and event listings, news, and local information.
- **Wisconsin Trails:** Ideal for nature lovers, this app includes details about the best trails in the state for hiking, biking, and more.

Useful Websites

- **Jack and Kitty:** We have hundreds (maybe thousands by the time you read this!) of articles with fun things to do in Wisconsin. Visit us to get inspired (www.jackandkitty.com)
- **Travel Wisconsin:** The official site of the Wisconsin Department of Tourism (www. travelwisconsin.com)
- **Wisconsin Department of Natural Resources:** Information about state parks, recreational activities, and conservation efforts (www.dnr.wi.gov)
- **Wisconsin Department of Transportation:** Road condition updates, travel information, and more (www.dot. wisconsin.gov)

Tourist Information Centers

- **Wisconsin Welcome Centers:** Found throughout the state, these centers offer travel information and advice.
- **Local Visitor Centers:** Many cities, including Madison and Milwaukee, have their own visitor centers.

Health and Safety

Always check the CDC and local public health department websites for up-to-date health and safety information, including COVID-19 guidelines.

Hospitals

- **University of Wisconsin Hospital (Madison)**
- **Froedtert Hospital & the Medical College of Wisconsin (Milwaukee)**
- **Aurora St. Luke's Medical Center (Milwaukee)**

Pharmacies

- **Walgreens:** With multiple locations statewide, Walgreens is a reliable choice for prescriptions and health products.

- **CVS:** Also found across Wisconsin, CVS offers pharmacy services in addition to a range of health, wellness, and personal care items.
- **Hometown Pharmacy:** A Wisconsin-based pharmacy chain with multiple locations.

Travel Insurance

Before embarking on your Wisconsin adventure, it's recommended to have travel insurance to cover any unexpected incidents. Check with your insurance provider for coverage options that suit your travel needs.

This chapter serves as a quick reference guide for vital information. With these resources, you'll be well-equipped to handle any situation during your visit to Wisconsin, ensuring a safe and pleasant journey through the Badger State.

Chapter 27

About the Authors

Jack and Kitty Norton are Emmy Award winning authors and bloggers. High school sweethearts turned married soulmates, this fun-loving couple lives in the small college town of Winona, Minnesota and would love to have you over for some tater tot hotdish.

Chapter 28

Connect with Jack and Kitty

We love sharing fun things to do in Wisconsin... and beyond! Please connect with us online for lots more fun travel tips and tricks to make the most out of your time in the Badger State.

Links

Travel Blog
Our travel blog is updated daily with articles and fun resources to help make your next trip awesome! Find it at:
JackAndKitty.com

Travel Videos on YouTube
Do we love making travel vids for Youtube? You betcha! Join us for video tours, hidden gems and history lessons all about the great state of Wisconsin! Subscribe at:
YouTube.com/@JackAndKitty

Write to Us!

Wanna share your favorite Wisconsin memories with us? A fun photo from your trip? Maybe some cheese curds? Hopefully cheese curds.

Jack and Kitty Norton
278 Mankato Ave, Suite 103
Winona, MN 55987
hello@jackandkitty.com

Suggestion or Correction?

Do you have a suggestion for a fun place to include in future editions of this book? Maybe you'd like us to write a blog article or make a video about a neat place in Wisconsin? We'd love to hear your ideas!

Also, we'll try to keep this book as up-to-date as possible, but if you have a correction or tip, please email us at: **hello@jackandkitty.com** - we appreciate your help and look forward to connecting with you!

If You Enjoyed This Book, Don't Miss the Helpful Articles on...

JackAndKitty.com

Find Out Why We're the Midwest's Favorite News Blog!

Wanna Explore More?

Don't miss these additional travel guidebooks from Jack and Kitty!

101 Bizarre, Quirky and Totally Fun Adventures in the Midwest

Minnesota's Best:
365 Unique Adventures

Iowa's Best:
365 Unique Adventures

Available in bookstores everywhere and at JackAndKitty.com

You Deserve to Feel-Good Today!

Uplifting Stories From the Heartland... to Your Heart!

Feel-Good Stories
for Dog Lovers

Christmas Feel-Good Stories:
Holidays in the Heartland

Feel-Good Stories
about Animals

Available in bookstores everywhere and at JackAndKitty.com